Greenhou

The Ultimate Guide to Achieving Your Dream Greenhouse

By Una Pitt

Copyright @2018 Una Pitt

All rights reserved. No part of this book may be reproduced in any form or by any means without permission in writing from the publisher, .

If you like my book, please leave a positive review on Amazon. I would appreciate it a lot. Thanks! This is the link:

Leave your review here. Thank you!

Contents

Chapter 1 - How Does A Greenhouse Capture Heat? 4

Chapter 2 - Sorts Of Greenhouses 6

Chapter 3 - Instruments And Materials For Your Greenhouse 8

Chapter 4 - Greenhouse Tables, Shelving And Plant Holders 10

Chapter 5 - Tips For Your Greenhouse 12

Chapter 6 - Take in The Benefits Of Greenhouse Gardening 15

Chapter 7 - Dealing with The Greenhouse Climate 19

Chapter 8 - Planting Inside The Greenhouse 23

Chapter 9 - Greenhouse Kits For Plant Enthusiasts 27

Chapter 10 - Make A Warm And Suitable Environment For Growth With Greenhouse Plastic 31

Chapter 11 - Greenhouses: Where The Grass Is Green All Year-Round 35

Chapter 12 - What Makes Up The Greenhouse Structure? 39

Chapter 13 - Know Your Greenhouse Supplies 43

Chapter 14 - Supplies Needed For Your Greenhouse 48

Chapter 15 - Supplies You'll Need For A More Productive Greenhouse 52

Chapter 16 - What Every Gardener Needs To Know About Greenhouse Systems 56

Chapter 17 - How Does A Greenhouse Work: The Benefits That Can Be Derived From Its Acts 60

Chapter 18 - The Purposes Of Hydroponics Greenhouses 64

Chapter 19 - What You Get From 'Lean-To' Greenhouses 68

Chapter 20 - Greenhouses Ideal For Small Areas 72

Chapter 21 - Considering Buying A Greenhouse? 76

Chapter 22 - Rules For Constructing Your Commercial Greenhouse 79

Chapter 23 - 5 Essentials For A Commercial Greenhouse 82

Chapter 24 - Business Greenhouse Kits 85
Chapter 25 - Free Greenhouse Plan For You 88
Chapter 26 - Greenhouse Accessories And Their Utility 91
Chapter 27 - Greenhouse Designs 95
Chapter 28 - Treating Greenhouse Plants 98
Chapter 29 - Treatment Of Greenhouse Crops............................... 101
Chapter 30 - Warming Up A Greenhouse....................................... 105
Chapter 31 - Keeping up Humidity Levels Inside A Greenhouse.. 108
Chapter 32 - 5 Factors To Consider When Choosing Greenhouse Lighting... 111
Chapter 33 - The Business Relationship Between Farmers And Greenhouse Manufacturers.. 115
Chapter 34 - Distinguishing The Best Greenhouse Manufacturer 118
Chapter 35 - Framing Up The Greenhouse..................................... 122
Chapter 36 - Picking And Comparing Greenhouse Panels............ 126
Chapter 37 - Picking A Window Greenhouse 130
Chapter 38 - Appreciating Greenhouse Gardening........................ 133
Chapter 39 - Building An Easy And Cost-compelling Greenhouse On Your Back Yard... 136
Chapter 40 - Greenhouses On The Move.. 139

Chapter 1 - How Does A Greenhouse Capture Heat?

A Greenhouse utilizes a unique sort of glass that goes about as a medium which specifically transmits ghostly frequencies. Unearthly originates from "range".

In layman's terms, a phantom recurrence can be characterized as far as the accompanying guideline: any protest in the universe produces, emanates or transmits light. The dispersion of this light along an electromagnetic range is controlled by the question's structure.

Consequently, the glass of a Greenhouse traps vitality inside the Greenhouse and the warmth thusly gives warmth to the plants and the ground inside the Greenhouse. It warms the air close to the ground, keeping it from rising and leaving the bounds of the structure.

For instance, on the off chance that you open a little window close to the top of a Greenhouse, the temperature drops altogether. This is a result of the auto vent programmed cooling framework. An autovent is essentially a gadget utilized by Greenhouses that keep up a scope of temperatures inside. This is the manner by which Greenhouses trap electromagnetic radiation and counteracts convection (transference of warmth by streams inside a liquid).

Inquisitive about how the possibility of a Greenhouse occurred? It backpedals to the times of the Romans, who - as history archives indicate - were the principal individuals to make a structure to ensure plants. Utilizing warmed pits, they set up sections of shake to frame crude Greenhouses. The term

"glasshouse" which is the right name of this structure, was embraced at some point in the seventeenth and eighteenth centuries.

Around then, be that as it may, the blunder was in trusting that warmth was more essential than light for plants to flourish. Structures were being worked to prohibit the section of light, yet when the glass duty of 1845 was nullified, the plan of Greenhouses began to change.

Developers acknowledged then that a bended rooftop rather than a level one permitted higher centralizations of the sun's beams, and that by utilizing iron rather than wood, the Greenhouse could be fundamentally strengthened and made equipped for retaining all the more light.

Chapter 2 - Sorts Of Greenhouses

After you conclude that you need to manufacture a Greenhouse, you need to choose next what write to fabricate. This ought not be a troublesome one to address, if you realize what sorts of plants you need to develop. You should answer inquiries, for example,

- What will my Greenhouse be basically utilized for?

- Do I need an expansive or little Greenhouse?

- Will the Greenhouse be the fundamental fascination of my garden?

- Is my garden presented to solid breezes?

- Are there youthful kids or wild creatures in the zone?

Factors, for example, cost and space will decide the sort of Greenhouse you construct. On the off chance that you do live in a blustery region, it might be worth to spend the additional cash for a strong and durable Greenhouse. On the off chance that you live close to an expansive handyman shop or a Greenhouse, or even a do-it-without anyone else's help home focus, go and visit a few models. The client benefit delegate ought to have the capacity to give you profitable data previously you settle on a ultimate choice.

So as not to misdirect you, while there might be distinctive kinds of Greenhouse outlines, we're discussing a similar Greenhouse. You get the chance to choose which write you need it to be. For instance, if temperature is the primary factor, on account of the plant assortments you need to develop, at that point there are three writes as far as temperature control. There are additionally unique kinds of Greenhouses in light of auxiliary plan. We'll begin with temperature control factors.

For temperature control purposes, three kinds of Greenhouses exist:

- A hot Greenhouse

- A warm Greenhouse

- A cool Greenhouse.

Chapter 3 - Instruments And Materials For Your Greenhouse

Keep in mind that you are not restricted to a specific assortment of plants to develop in a Greenhouse. Remember, in any case, that your inclination for specific natural products, vegetables and plants will decide the kind of Greenhouse you get a kick out of the chance to fabricate. "Know thy edit" is a critical factor before settling on the Greenhouse compose you will introduce.

You will require a decent soil for planting seeds. Manure, preparing or cultivating soil and a little sand or perlite are a decent begin. Read all bearings in your seed bundles.

Keep some of those dark plastic pads that Greenhouses use to show their plant compartments. These are valuable for beginning sees and transplants.

Seats in Greenhouses are basic, as they hold plate of plants that have effectively grown from seeds.

Styrofoam mugs - have a few of these convenient. Seeds grow rapidly and once they develop sufficiently huge to move into partitioned holders, they can be delicately lifted and moved into standard Styrofoam containers.

You can likewise utilize yogurt plastic glasses, and extensive business compose compartments that can hold more than one plant. Truth be told, any holder you can consider will be reasonable.

Different materials you ought to have close by are broken dirt pots, split walnuts, marbles, charcoal or rock. These assistance in legitimate seepage. Make sure to absorb earth pots water a couple of minutes before utilizing them. This will keep the earth from retaining the dampness from the gardening soil.

In the event that you need to have trellises inside your Greenhouse, you can influence them to out of coat holders, which you can twist to any shape your heart wants.

Herbs are ideal for keeping bugs under control. They are what one author calls "nature's bug sprays". Have an assortment of them inside your Greenhouse. You can make a characteristic bug spray by adding onions or garlic to a jug of water. Abandon it for a week and shower on your plants.

Other garden instruments that will enable you to run your Greenhouse proficiently are air coolers for the sweltering summer. This is to keep up the temperatures at wanted levels. Power vents in the rooftop are likewise a smart thought to discharge sweltering air that can develop all of a sudden in the late spring.

Chapter 4 - Greenhouse Tables, Shelving And Plant Holders

These are basic, particularly when you have to work inside your Greenhouse and to amplify and sort out your Greenhouse space. As your plant assortments develop, you will require retires and tables and plant holders to encourage your cultivating. One famous sort of seat that Greenhouse specialists like is the cedar twofold layer seat. They are solid and proficient to utilize.

For racks, you can decide on two and three area lengths made of aluminum

Given that watering your plants is a fundamental - basic - part of any Greenhouse cultivating, a great watering framework is required. You can pick either the programmed or hand held watering framework to make your watering needs more proficient.

For programmed water system frameworks, there are models that come outfitted with a programmed dribble water system and manure framework. Day or night, they frequently water the plants and modify the stream of compost. Some have a tank in which the water and compost are blended and are appropriated to plants by means of hoses, Y-connections and dribble pins.

Greenhouse cultivate curl indoor/open air watering wand

This is a "self-curling" garden hose made of tough and solid polyurethane tubing. It produces ultra-fine fogs and showers in delicate, delicate streams. Some wand models reach out to as long as 50 feet. No issue stockpiling due to self-winding system.

Greenhouses continually advance in style and outline. It takes after then that devices and adornments will develop in number or existing ones will be significantly moved forward. Makers are presumably imagining more devices and adornments this exact second that will make our work in Greenhouses less demanding and faster.

The ones we simply depicted are as of now being utilized by numerous Greenhouse devotees. In a couple of years, new items will show up in the market.

Chapter 5 - Tips For Your Greenhouse

In case you're developing carrots, beets, turnips and other root crops, they flourish well in profound boxes which can be put under seats. Those that require tub-type holders are tomatoes, peas, cucumbers and shaft beans, while lettuce, or other low verdant vegetables might be planted in the tub with the taller vegetables.

You can plant corn straight onto the floor of the Greenhouse, in an uncommon bed arranged for it. To spare space, you can plant pumpkin between the lines of corn.

Utilize room temperature water to water your indoor plants. Give tap a chance to water remain for a day to dispose of the chlorine substance. Along these lines you evade your plants getting darker tips.

Circulate pulverized egg shells in your garden to animate development. Sprinkling espresso beans will add corrosive to the Greenhouse ground.

Before bringing vegetables and natural products from the Greenhouse to your home, flush them well outside; along these lines soil and bugs remain outside and won't influence your kitchen to filthy.

To make more space in your Greenhouse, utilize bring down seats for beginning seeds and transplants; upper seats for developing blossoms and example plants. A few vegetables, similar to tomatoes, ought to be planted in a warm segment of the Greenhouse.

With respect to of seeds, make certain to water daintily for the initial couple of times. Over watering may make the seeds rise to the top too early, keeping them from establishing legitimately.

Readiness and generation must be done in particular zones. Try not to do general readiness on the developing floor. This makes for a tidier Greenhouse.

Here is a rundown of the biggest vegetables that will require the most separating in your Greenhouse:

- Bush type beans: least of five feet between columns,

- Cabbage: a foot between columns,

- Peppers: about a foot between columns,

- Cantaloupes: a few feet between columns,

- Squash: a few feet between columns,

- Tomatoes and watermelons: least of two feet between columns.

Chapter 6 - Take in The Benefits Of Greenhouse Gardening

Greenhouse cultivating can appear a little outdated nowadays. It is so natural to hop in the auto and drive to the general store where we can locate each sort of products of the soil flown in from everywhere throughout the world. You need crisp strawberries in winter? Don't sweat it, there they are on the rack. May be you require some green beans for supper. Get a little plastic wrapped plate that were growing three days back in Kenya.

Be that as it may, these are the very purposes behind moving to Greenhouse planting. Driving and flying consume progressively rare non-renewable energy sources and discharge ozone harming substances into the climate. An ever increasing number of individuals are awakening to the threats of a worldwide temperature alteration.

Crisp foods grown from the ground have never been less demanding to purchase than they are today. We live during a time of comfort and prompt delight. A Greenhouse appears to involve just an excessive amount of work and the satisfaction is delayed for a really long time. Greenhouses appear to be inconsequential until the point when we start to consider the more extensive picture and the sort of world our youngsters and grandchildren will acquire.

Getting into Greenhouse planting can be a biologically and socially dependable decision. You will eat products of the soil that have developed in your own particular terrace. They have not been flown mostly round the planet to get to your plate. What's more you didn't need to drive to get them. You took a short walk and got some solid exercise each day when you exited to the Greenhouse to keep an eye on them.

We have used to those helpful little bundles in the store. We like having our vegetables prepared arranged and washed. In any case, we have likewise got used to poor taste. The leafy foods we purchase in the general store have lost the majority of their regular sugars that give them their flavor. Indeed, even the assortments are decided for their time span of usability as opposed to their flavor.

When you encounter home developed products of the soil straight from the Greenhouse you will enter another nature of flavor. A new picked tomato detonates in your mouth with season. Becoming your own particular in the Greenhouse implies that you can choose assortments that have the best flavor.

An entire scope of uncommon assortments exist that are once in a while developed financially are accessible to you with a Greenhouse. With your own Greenhouse you can investigate these lesser known assortments of recognizable products of the soil. You can even turn out to be extremely gutsy and attempt the sorts of products of the soil that you just get in authority stores.

A Greenhouse opens the world to you as opposed to conveying it to you at incredible cost to the planet and everybody on it. Your carbon impression will be littler however your points of view will be more extensive.

"In any case, I don't have time." I hear you say and it is genuine we are largely shy of time. Be that as it may, a brief period spent in the Greenhouse has colossal individual advantages. It is unimaginably remedial to go into the Greenhouse in the wake of a monotonous day and simply work discreetly for a hour or something like that. Investing energy with developing things is a perceived remedy to discouragement and nervousness. A Greenhouse is a sedative with no reactions aside from a more advantageous eating regimen.

In the event that you have children, what better approach to invest some quality energy with them than in the Greenhouse. It gives you and them unpressured time to talk. You are occupied with a joint undertaking. A Greenhouse can turn into a holding knowledge for the family.

There is the additional advantage that working with you in the Greenhouse gives them the sort of handy hands on lesson that is from time to time gave in school. They are finding out about how things develop. Every session in the Greenhouse is a science lesson in itself. They are finding out about the plants and about the creepy crawlies that feast upon them and fertilize them.

They, and you, will take in a great deal about natural science when you blend your plant nourishments, bug sprays and different chemicals. You will without a doubt take in a considerable measure about gadgets and taking care of essential devices as you gain the power frameworks of your Greenhouse working and apparatus up plant backings and water system channels.

A kid who discovers scholarly lessons a troublesome will regularly sparkle at errands they can learn by involvement. Plants are exceptionally sympathetic and even youngsters who endure with issues of fixation can encounter the fulfillment of accomplishment growing a couple of basic harvests in the Greenhouse

Chapter 7 - Dealing with The Greenhouse Climate

Dealing with the atmosphere of a Greenhouse is tied in with giving the plants the correct conditions for development, blossoming and fruiting. What you have to do will in this manner rely upon the sort of plants you are developing and the stage they have come to in their life cycle.

Not all plants require the very same conditions so the sort of atmosphere will rely upon what you intend to develop in you Greenhouse. Some will require high temperatures and high mugginess in the Greenhouse. Others will require somewhat cooler conditions in the Greenhouse.

It is regularly conceivable to achieve a trade off and give conditions that will suit the greater part of your plants more often than not. You won't have the capacity to give ideal conditions to every one of the plants in your Greenhouse. Yet, by picking plants that like comparable conditions you will accomplish satisfactory outcomes.

For the novice Greenhouse producer a few bargains are vital. In the event that you are developing industrially that is another issue. A business Greenhouse must give an ideal atmosphere to a particular sort of plant. Else you will lose cash.

A novice who is devoted to a specific animal types needs to settle on some hard decisions. It might be important to forfeit assortment for quality. On the off chance that your Greenhouse is committed to orchids and just orchids you can give the best climatic conditions. In the event that you need to develop different sorts of plant you will simply need to fabricate another Greenhouse.

For most cultivators such hard choices are a bit much. It is conceivable to give an atmosphere that will suit numerous plants to some degree. You may likewise find that you can parcel off piece of the Greenhouse to make a microclimate. Some portion of the Greenhouse would then be able to have an atmosphere that is more smoking or more muggy than the rest.

In a mild piece of the planet where there is a moderately long developing season it is frequently conceivable to have an unheated Greenhouse. An unheated Greenhouse depends on the sun's beams and the lingering heat put away in the ground to make an atmosphere that is hotter than the outside condition. This is satisfactory for raising seeds and for developing vegetables, for example, tomatoes in the late spring.

Controlling the atmosphere in an unheated Greenhouse is for the most part a matter of ensuring that there is sufficient stickiness to maintain a strategic distance from bugs, for example, white fly and red arachnid bug and enough ventilation to evade buildup and botrytis. The lower the Temperature the lower the stickiness ought to be. Air can't hold much dampness at low temperature and decay will come about if the Greenhouse isn't appropriately ventilated.

Giving some warmth will permit a more drawn out developing season. On the off chance that the Greenhouse is warmed in the winter it will be conceivable to give an ice free space to delicate plants that live outside in the late spring. A little measure of warmth will give a Greenhouse atmosphere in which a few servings of mixed greens can be developed all dread round.

The most straightforward strategy for accomplishing an ice free Greenhouse is the outdated one of setting a light in a vast plant pot with another over the best. The plant pots warm up and keep on giving out warmth as the night progressed. Your Greenhouse will be without ice in a few degrees of ice. On the off chance that you expect to keep your Greenhouse warmed throughout the day or if the atmosphere in your area is extremely frosty in winter you should put resources into a more mind boggling type of warming. Electric warming is by a wide margin the best choice. It can be thermostatically controlled to create precisely the atmosphere you require.

Electric warming is costly, yet you can lessen warm misfortune by protecting your Greenhouse with bubble wrap plastic. This is a similar sort of material that is utilized as a part of bundling. You can get it in huge sheets from cultivate providers. When it is cut to within the Greenhouse it makes a twofold coated condition.

Protecting a Greenhouse enables you to keep up higher temperatures in your Greenhouse. Be that as it may, you should be cautious about mugginess. Some ventilation will even now be essential. Venting the Greenhouse amidst the day will control the inner atmosphere. Less expensive types of warming exist yet any sort of ignition definitely delivers gases that are destructive to plants. They are best maintained a strategic distance from. In the event that you have a lot of wood then you should think about a wood consuming stove. As opposed to put such a stove specifically in the Greenhouse it is smarter to utilize it as a focal warming stove and pipe high temp water through your Greenhouse.

Chapter 8 - Planting Inside The Greenhouse

A Greenhouse speaks to a noteworthy speculation for generally plant specialists. Indeed, even the littlest and least complex sorts of Greenhouse don't come shabby nowadays. They likewise request a venture of your opportunity. So for what reason should you think about a Greenhouse.

Maybe the principle favorable position of a Greenhouse is that is furnishes the plant specialist with a more drawn out developing season. This is especially vital in colder territories. A Greenhouse will give a promising start to seedlings, hotter conditions for delicate plants and an ice free condition for plants that won't make due out of entryways.

Another, less frequently perceived, advantage is that a Greenhouse enables a planter with portability issues to cultivate at table stature in warm conditions. Plants can be raised to a helpful stature for the Greenhouse worker in a Greenhouse. Straightforward arranging, either home made or purchased for the reason will make a situation in which an impaired Greenhouse worker can appreciate every one of the delights of planting without bending or extend or get chilled.

A Greenhouse can turn into a most loved place to sit and appreciate whatever remains of your garden. On a frosty winter day the Greenhouse will keep the breeze of and give a shielded spot to consider one year from now's designs.

What you utilize a Greenhouse for will rely upon your very own inclinations. Lovely shows of mountains can be made in a Greenhouse on seats secured with rock. It might appear to be interesting to develop plants that are basically tough in a Greenhouse yet it bodes well. Peaks hate to get wet. They are accustomed to being solidified all winter however won't survive soggy conditions. Their blossoms are regularly little and can best be acknowledged when set on a seat.

Summer bedding plants and vegetable seeds can be brought up in an unheated Greenhouse. In the event that you need to abstain from paying high costs for prepared developed plants a Greenhouse might be the appropriate response. You can develop numerous a larger number of plants from a bundle of seeds than you could bear to purchase. Your garden will turn into an uproar of shading as you try different things with new yearly sheet material plans, hanging containers and grower.

Vegetables will achieve development prior in the event that you bring you seeds up in a Greenhouse. Your products will be prepared before out entryway sown plants are prepared for gathering. With all plants sown in the Greenhouse you should be mindful so as to solidify them to outside conditions gradually. Put them outside when the danger of ice has passed. Do this amid the day at first. As they get used to the colder conditions you can forget them around evening time. When you are certain they are sufficiently solid plant them in their last position.

At this point you will be prepared to consider what you need to develop in your Greenhouse amid the late spring. You may wish to develop foods grown from the ground. Tomatoes and cucumbers or melons are dependably top picks. They are similarly simple to develop. These can be developed without warm.

On the off chance that you need to utilize your Greenhouse in the winter you should give warming. Maybe the best type of warming in a little novice Greenhouse is an electric warmer. This can be controlled by an indoor regulator which will manage the temperature in the Greenhouse. The indoor regulator can be set at the coveted temperature. Managing the temperature is the most ideal approach to keep a mind the cost of warming.

For over wintering plants that become outside in the mid year however are not winter solid the temperature just should be set simply above solidifying. A couple of degrees of warmth will keep up delicate plants in a semi-torpid state until the point when you can return them to the garden.

To keep utilizing your Greenhouse for plants and blooms that are in development you will require higher temperatures. Summer plants can be developed throughout the entire year along these lines. On the off chance that you will warm your Greenhouse to developing temperatures around 60 or 70 degrees Fahrenheit you should consider protecting the Greenhouse with bubble wrap plastic.

It might be important to give extra lighting in the event that you are at a northern scope with short winter day lengths. Plants require light notwithstanding warmth and moistness. Plants require light and also warmth. Some of them require particular day lengths before they come into bloom. Lighting enables you to control the condition totally. This is the means by which business cultivators get blossoms into sprout time for Christmas.

Chapter 9 - Greenhouse Kits For Plant Enthusiasts

Indeed, even the least complex Greenhouse can be costly and instant ones are from time to time exactly what we need. An instant Greenhouse may not fit our plot or may not give sufficiently very space to what we intend to develop. Building your own particular Greenhouse from a unit may the best choice for some planters.

So in the event that you are attempting to a tight spending plan or dream of a specially crafted Greenhouse a unit might be only the thing you require. The level of aptitude included is inside the scope of a large portion of us. On the off chance that you can do basic assignments around the home and take after fundamental guidelines then you can most likely collect a Greenhouse from a unit.

As a matter of first importance you should consider what you need from your Greenhouse. How should it look? In the event that you need a rich plan that will look great, at that point one of the redwood Greenhouse packs may the thing for you. Investigate the Sunshine go. These are produced using strong redwood outlines with polycarbonate coating.

This sort of Greenhouse pack is anything but difficult to gather on the grounds that the coating is incorporated with the edge, so you have no slicing to do. Cutting glass is a precarious business. Fitting glass into a casing is significantly more troublesome and you may have numerous softened sheets previously you prevail up getting a solid match. Polycarbonate is likewise sheltered. This is particularly imperative when there are youngsters about.

Redwood Greenhouse packs are great decision. The disadvantage is their cost. They extend from $1000 to $4000.

In the event that financial plan is an essential thought for you investigate aluminum surrounded Greenhouse units. These range in cost from $2,500 to £30,000. At the lower end of the range you may discover an outline that suits your requirements. They are less rich than the redwood Greenhouse units however Cross Country run are exceptionally very much composed and will give a long time of planting administration.

Estimated at $1000 to $2000 there is the Hobby Gardener scope of Greenhouse packs. These have "snapless" boards made of polycarbonate. They give a decent tallness that makes working in them simple and a lot of room for the plants. Their pivoted entryway and vent framework enable the Greenhouse worker to make a perfect microclimate inside the Greenhouse.

As far as highlights, for example, entryways and venting aluminum and readwood packs are practically identical. They are built to exclusive expectations. An aluminum outline Greenhouse will never look as wonderful as a redwood one however they have the preferred standpoint that the casing needs no upkeep. Once an aluminum

Greenhouse is manufactured that is all you need to do. from the Greenhouse worker's perspective they are sans inconvenience.

Additionally useful for those with restricted spending plans is the Juliana scope of Greenhouse units. These are made of aluminum outlines and have twin divider polycarbonate coating. They begin as low as $65 settling on them a perfect decision at the cost cognizant. For those on an extremely tight spending plan the Little Greenhouse scope of packs might be the perfect alternative. These Greenhouse packs are secured with four millimeter polyethylene sheeting on a PVC outline. They are less sturdy than the sorts of Greenhouse units as of now talked about however they are more temperate and useful for the learner.

On the off chance that you are not yet beyond any doubt in the event that you need to make a major venture of time and cash then a Little Greenhouse pack might be a decent beginning stage. Maybe you don't expect to remain long at your present home and would prefer not to focus on a costly structure. They are even valuable in the event that you as of now have a more perpetual Greenhouse yet need that additional piece of room. This sort of Greenhouse unit might be the perfect one for a wide range of reasons.

On the off chance that you have to cover an extensive territory and the presence of the structure isn't critical to you then you could attempt a convenient Greenhouse. These are made of a steel outline secured with plastic sheeting. You can get these for as meager as

$300. They resemble the business polytunnels they are however the leisure activity cultivator can put them to great utilize. Inside you can make a tropical heaven on the off chance that you utilize a twofold layer of polythene.

Polythene is dependably a shoddy alternative for a Greenhouse unit. In any case, is does not have the toughness of polycarbonate or the light transmission properties. A polythene cover should be changed each year or somewhere in the vicinity. Polycarbonate will keep going for quite a long time. Also twin walled polycarbonate lessens warming expenses since it gives protection and guarantees less warmth misfortune to the outside condition.

Chapter 10 - Make A Warm And Suitable Environment For Growth With Greenhouse Plastic

Plastic in all its numerous structures has to a great extent supplanted glass in the garden. In addition to the fact that it is more secure, a vital thought when there are youngsters about, yet it has better warm properties and regularly transmits all the more light.

What you are endeavoring to accomplish by utilizing Greenhouse plastic is a microclimate suited to your plants. You are shielding them from the rigors of the outside condition. You are guarding them from ice, low temperatures, wind and rain.

In a desolate recognize the Greenhouse worker can utilize Greenhouse plastic to shield plants from drying out caused by the breeze. In a mild however soggy atmosphere an all around ventilated Greenhouse will permit peaks which lean toward icy dry conditions and great light to flourish. In northern scopes similar materials can be utilized for tropical and semi-tropical plants or to give solid plants an ambitious start.

The benefit of present day plastic materials is that a similar Greenhouse innovation can be connected broadly in the garden. There is no compelling reason to keep yourself to a customary Greenhouse structure. You may utilize Greenhouse plastic in an impermanent structure that spreads some portion of the garden for a couple of long stretches of the year. Similarly you can utilize plastic to build a detailed lasting Greenhouse.

The most broadly utilized plastics are PVC, polyethylene and copolymers. Each of these sorts of plastic has its own properties and employments. They all be cut effortlessly and don't smash which used to be the issue with glass in the Greenhouse. This enables them to be utilized as a part of inventive structures or redid to fit clumsy spaces.

While picking plastic for a Greenhouse it is critical to decide on a high review material that will withstand wear and tear. Poor quality plastic will fall apart when presented to the earth and turn out to be progressively dark. The plastic utilized as a part of a Greenhouse must transmit light well. A few plastics may should be supplanted following a year. So go for a plastic that is particularly intended for Greenhouse utilize. It will last more.

Plastic that will be utilized as a part of a Greenhouse should be impervious to debasement by bright radiation. Numerous plastics are debilitated by bright radiation and will tear effectively after some time.

On the off chance that you need long haul use out of plastic sheeting pick a strengthened kind. This is particularly vital if wind harm is an inquiry. Then again utilize an inflexible plastic. Twin divider polycarbonate is a perfect decision for a more lasting structure. It has the additional preferred standpoint of giving protection since air is caught between the two dividers.

At the point when utilized as a part of a regular Greenhouse twin divider polycarbonate looks like glass yet will lessen your warming bills. It is a sort of moment twofold coating. It has cut down the cost of Greenhouse planting and brought the real hot house inside the compass of the leisure activity planter. It is never again restrictively costly to warm your Greenhouse to high temperatures in the winter.

Plastic has truly reformed Greenhouse development. No where is this more valid than with adaptable plastic sheeting. This material has permitted crops like strawberries to be developed all the year round even in northern scopes. Polytunnels have turned out to be far reaching in business cultivation.

A similar business innovation is progressively getting to be plainly accessible to the specialist. It is conceivable to purchase a similar steel outline, plastic sheeting that the experts utilize. The casings deliver an unattached passage structure over which plastic is extended and secured with extraordinary clasps. A scope of sizes are accessible and the littler sizes are perfect for novice utilize.

A passage of this write enables a huge zone to be secured relatively inexpensively. A whole vegetable plot can be shrouded along these lines financially.

Maybe the principle favorable position of such a structure is its transitory nature. The entire thing can be destroyed and moved or put away until one year from now. The specialist at that point has the upside of a Greenhouse without devoting some portion of the plot to a structure that is just used to the full for a short piece of the year.

A passage molded steel outline shrouded in plastic isn't the most delightful question. Numerous individuals would like to keep it out sight of the house. Yet, it gives tremendous and still to a great extent unexplored potential outcomes for decorative subjects. A twofold layer of plastic will give protection. Temperatures would then be able to be raised to hot house levels and a scope of tropical plants developed.

It is conceivable to make a naturalistic tropical condition thusly. A little water highlight will raise the stickiness and enable the plants to develop in a way that they never can in the dry condition of a house. Fish and different animals can be added to finish the tropical scene.

By utilizing present day plastic materials you can make a Greenhouse situation that would once have been past the financial plan of the vast majority.

Chapter 11 - Greenhouses: Where The Grass Is Green All Year-Round

The winter comes. The evenings attract and we overlook the decking and the yard until the spring. Yet, in the Greenhouse it is summer all year. With a Greenhouse it is conceivable to have a little bit of summer that stays with us through the dull winter nights and the snow.

Warming a Greenhouse used to be a costly business. In any case, with present day materials that is never again obvious. It is presently conceivable to warm a Greenhouse financially. What was before an extravagance is accessible to everybody.

A twin divider polycarbonate Greenhouse is twofold coated and will keep in the warmth. You can utilize an electric radiator that is controlled by an indoor regulator. Almost no warmth will escape into the outside condition. Via deliberately directing the temperature it is conceivable to monitor the bills.

On the off chance that you keep the temperature a little above solidifying you can develop plants that like genuinely cool temperature. A show of cyclamen, for instance, would be a pleasure. When we keep them in our homes they effectively get excessively hot. An ice free Greenhouse would be perfect for them. You can acquire maybe a couple to the house for a day or two preceding returning them to the Greenhouse to be resuscitated in the cooler temperature.

There are an entire scope of plants that are sold as house plants in any case despise the dry climate. Think about every one of those exquisite plants that bite the dust following fourteen days. Crotons with their wonderful leaves or Schizanthus, the poor man's orchid or butterfly blossom, as it is once in a while known, they cherish dampness. In a Greenhouse you can give them the conditions they require.

Numerous dynamite plants, for example, the feathered creature of heaven bloom, or the strelizia, just need evening temperature of 55 degrees Fahrenheit. That isn't difficult to accomplish. In the day time the sun will raise the temperature for you. You will require day time warming on just a couple of days of the year.

Put one of your garden seats in the Greenhouse and stay there in the winter sun tuning in to some music encompassed by blossoms and greenery. The considerable thing about a Greenhouse is you can utilize it practically anyway you need.

I know individuals who keep angle in their Greenhouses. A little pool effortlessly solidifies over on the off chance that you have hard winters in your piece of the world. You can lose your fish that way. In the Greenhouse the water remains free of ice and you can nourish your prize koi carp directly through the winter.

Inside fashioners frequently discuss carrying the garden into the house. All things considered, with a Greenhouse you are truly intermixing Greenhouse and house. Your Greenhouse can turn into a room committed to plants or an expansion of the garden.

In any case, perhaps the kitchen is more your thing and you need to develop leafy foods trims in your Greenhouse. You need the essence of new picked create directly through the winter. That should be possible as well.

You can develop a wide range of yields in you Greenhouse. Plates of mixed greens are most likely the least demanding of all. New lettuce, rocket, spinach and different leaves can be developed on a cut and come back again premise. Herbs should be possible a similar way. All you need to would when you like to make a plate of mixed greens is to fly out to the Greenhouse and draw a couple of clears out.

Serving of mixed greens goes up against another measurement when it is that new. Simply keep an overcoat or an umbrella by the kitchen entryway. Tomatoes are likewise easy to become through the winter. They require warm. They jump at the chance to be around 70 degrees.

You ought to likewise consider lighting on the off chance that you need to develop trims in the winter. Most foods grown from the ground require longer day lengths than a northern winter permits. Bright lights are genuinely great and modest to run yet you will get the best outcomes from grolights that copy the range of characteristic sunshine. They are metal halide or high weight sodium lights that have a reflector to build the measure of light. You can likewise make reflectors to go round the plants from conventional aluminum heating foil. That can be a goof thought notwithstanding when you are depending on daylight in the winter.

Whatever you are developing in your Greenhouse you should consider ventilation. You require the air to travel through the Greenhouse. In the winter when you need to moderate warmth this should be possible with a ventilation fan. They are much the same as the ones utilized as a part of kitchens and lavatories or in cooker hoods. You can alter one of those in the event that you are helpful with apparatuses or get one that is reason made for the Greenhouse.

On the off chance that you truly need to save warm you can fit an adaptable hose to the vent and encourage the ousted air once more into the Greenhouse. For additional impact you can run the hose into a pit loaded with dark rocks. The warm air will warm up the stones which will go about as a capacity radiator, gradually emitting heat as the night progressed.

So whether you go for a Greenhouse that is a place to sit and watch the plants and angle or a Greenhouse that is expected to create trims there are great motivations to consider Greenhouse cultivating.

Chapter 12 - What Makes Up The Greenhouse Structure?

The development of Greenhouses has been upset by the coming of present day plastics. A scope of potential outcomes are accessible that would have been obscure previously.

Greenhouses were once made of wood and glass and even cast iron and glass. These materials spoke to an emotional mechanical improvement in their chance. Presently these conventional materials are an irregularity. They are safeguarded in the grounds of stately homes and exemplary professional flowerbeds.

The landing of aluminum made Greenhouses accessible to a more extensive market after World War Two. They were as yet coated with glass and nearly costly. Be that as it may, the interest for the leisure activity Greenhouse had started.

While superb leisure activity Greenhouses are frequently made of value timber, for example, redwood the most widely recognized kind of Greenhouse structure for the novice is made of aluminum. A timber casing will dependably look better. The feel of the aluminum structure uncover its causes in business agriculture. To numerous individuals they are unappealing, if practical.

Business Greenhouses are still frequently in view of aluminum structures, however the coating material has changed. Greenhouses are normally coated with twin divider polycarbonate nowadays. This material has the favorable position that is less expensive than glass and does not break. It likewise gives preferable warm protection over glass. The air caught between the two dividers shields warmth from getting away into the outside condition.

Indeed, even the edge of a Greenhouse might be made of plastic. The capability of UPVC, an inflexible plastic material that is impervious to bright radiation, was first perceived in the development business. It is utilized for entryways and twofold coated windows. A similar framework has now spread to Greenhouses. Standard units of twofold coating, or made to gauge boards, are made in a processing plant and conveyed to the site where they can be darted together.

The utilization of new materials has enabled new outlines of Greenhouse structure to be investigated. A Greenhouse used to be a rectangular structure regularly with a pitched rooftop. This was a useful outline is still generally utilized. Yet, the arch formed Greenhouse has turned out to be progressively well known. Regularly called a sun powered vault, this sort of structure makes the most utilization of light.

Vault molded Greenhouses were built out of solid metal in the nineteenth century. They were an extraordinary extravagance. They were regularly utilized as palm houses. Surviving illustrations are dynamite and uncommon structures.

Aluminum permitted arch formed Greenhouse to be mass delivered out of the blue. A similar shape would now be able to be found in redwood outlines as well. Greenhouses of this compose are frequently utilized as sun rooms and to cover pools in frosty atmospheres. On a huge scale a similar idea of a vault shape has been for the celebrated Eden Project biomes in Britain. The system of these structures is made of steel. Three goliath vault molded Greenhouses cover a recovered china earth pit and give a progression of situations that mirror the decent variety of the planet.

No less outwardly dynamite, in its own specific manner, is the humble polytunnel. This is a Greenhouse structure made of plastic sheeting extended over a steel system. Greenhouses of this write are generally utilized financially. There are such huge numbers of them in Southern Spain that they can be seen from space. Satellite pictures indicate vast territories of the locale covered with polytunnels.

Their business utilizes are evident however they the polytunnel can likewise be utilized as a part of an indistinguishable path from the more fantastic Greenhouses of the Eden Project. The Alternative Technology Center in Wales has a polytunnel planted with a scope of tropical plants. A little water include gives dampness to the plants. The entire impact is of a tranquil and rich tropical condition.

At a more straightforward level the utilization of plastics has made the likelihood of a more prominent scope of impermanent structures than was conceivable previously. It is conceivable to fabricate. or then again purchase instant, a tremendous scope of impermanent plastic Greenhouses that will fit into the littlest space. Indeed, even individuals who have just a gallery or porch would now be able to have a Greenhouse.

Since the Greenhouse is never again limited to the less difficult rectangular structure it is conceivable to adjust them a wide range of room. Present day plastic materials can be cut, twisted and extended in ways that would have been unthinkable with glass. The adjustment in Greenhouse structure and the accessibility of new materials has made the Greenhouse more available than any other time in recent memory.

Chapter 13 - Know Your Greenhouse Supplies

Once your Greenhouse is set up everything appears to be prepared to go. All you need to do in put in a few plants and there is no reason to worry. Be that as it may, this isn't the situation. You are exactly toward the start of a lengthy, difficult experience of experimentation.

You can dodge some costly oversights by arranging what sort of provisions you require. The greatest error is simply to purchase the most recent and fanciest device you find in the inventory. Set aside some opportunity to arrange for what you require.

Picking Greenhouse supplies relies upon what sort of Greenhouse you have and what you expect to develop in it. Set aside opportunity to consider what you truly require.

A few supplies will just fit in a specific make or state of Greenhouse. Others will be perfect for a few plants however for nobody else.

You should start this procedure of arranging even before you pick what sort of Greenhouse to purchase. That way you can purchase the fundamental things in the meantime as you purchase the Greenhouse. There might be cut value bargains here.

It is conceivable to fall back on home made arrangements. Be that as it may, in the event that you have a wonderful redwood display you truly need to remember the style. A weak arrangement of plant backings may work flawlessly well however won't look in the same class as the one your Greenhouse producer offers.

Choose what you will develop and how you will develop it. On the off chance that you expect to plant specifically into the earth you won't require seats of arranging as it called. This strategy is regularly utilized for plants like tomatoes, squashes, cucumbers and melons where tallness is critical.

Most Greenhouses advantage from some organizing. It is helpful for seedlings and littler plants. Aluminum organizing is accessible reasonably efficiently. It is tough and light on the off chance that you need to move it. In any case, it won't look great in a redwood Greenhouse where you ought to go for organizing made of timber. The entire impact will be better.

On the off chance that you have a bizarrely molded Greenhouse, for example, a sun based arch, regular arranging may not fit it. For this situation it is best to purchase a reason made framework provided for this sort of Greenhouse.

Something that few individuals consider when they start to utilize a Greenhouse is shading. The motivation behind a Greenhouse it to augment the warmth of the sun. It appears to be unreasonable to discuss the significance of shade. Be that as it may, shade is imperative in light of the fact that the sun can consume your plants.

Shading takes an assortment of structures. It can be accomplished by painting the glass with exceptional paint which can be washed off in the winter. A superior arrangement is shade netting which is cut to the structure of the Greenhouse. This is a comment with your producer who may offer a framework intended for your Greenhouse. A similar framework may likewise be utilized for plant bolsters.

The following inquiry is how would you expect to water your plants. You can, obviously, exit to the Greenhouse with a watering can. Be that as it may, in the tallness of the developing season you would need to do this few times each day.

A great many people lean toward a programmed watering framework. They work in various ways. Some work by bolstering water through a progression of dribble sustains in a pipe. This strategy is perfect for plants in pots. Others work by spreading water through a permeable hose. This technique is useful for plants developing in specifically in the earth. You will require an open air water supply to set up either framework in your Greenhouse.

Watering frameworks of either write can be controlled with a clock that fits onto the water supply. It kills the fawcett on an at the interims you set. A framework like this enables you to leave the Greenhouse while you are on an excursion.

An option is a uninvolved watering framework. This strategy utilizes slim tangling to draw water from a supply. A length of guttering settled along the edge of the seat will function admirably. The fine tangling is hung over the edge of the seat into the water and laid under the plants. The tangling must be kept secured to counteract it drying out. Rock or dark plastic can be utilized. Insofar as the supply is full your plants will be watered. The detriment of this strategy is that if the repository runs dry while you are away your plants will bite the dust.

By watering, ventilation is the real issue in Greenhouses. In the stature of summer a Greenhouse can turn out to be excessively sweltering. The most straightforward response to this issue is to open the entryway. Most Greenhouses accompany opening vents in the rooftop or dividers. A current of air traveling through the Greenhouse will hold the temperature down and stop nuisances, for example, whitefly.

Programmed frameworks that will open vents when the Greenhouse temperature achieves a specific level are accessible. You may likewise need to consider a more detailed arrangement and fit a fan. A fan may not be vital in the event that you are just utilizing your Greenhouse in the mid year, yet in the event that you need to utilize it amid the winter a fan is important. It will enable you to ventilate the Greenhouse and keep warm in. The air removed by the fan can even be recycled by fitting an adaptable hose to vent and returning it to the Greenhouse.

Developing in the winter requests lighting particularly in northern scopes. Plants require lights and also warmth and dampness to develop. A few plants will just come into bloom if the day length is right. Introducing lighting enables you to make a misleadingly taxing day.

Be that as it may, in the event that you are not wanting to develop plants in your Greenhouse amid the winter there is no need lighting. This is a region you can influence investment funds on Greenhouse supplies on the off chance that you to design ahead of time what you plan to develop.

The same is valid for warming. On the off chance that you need to utilize you Greenhouse amid the winter you will require some type of warming. An electric fan warmer is the best decision much of the time. Warming or lighting requires a power supply. You should consider this at a beginning period. It might impact where you position your Greenhouse.

Chapter 14 - Supplies Needed For Your Greenhouse

Greenhouse providers' lists are loaded with superb contraptions and must-have gadgets for your Greenhouse. In any case, what is extremely basic? Give us a chance to consider what sort of provisions you truly require.

And no more essential level you can escape with a watering can and a lot of time. On the off chance that you can exit to your Greenhouse a few times each day to water your plants and check the ventilation then you don't have to purchase anything. You may require the activity. Consider it a wellbeing cure.

Be that as it may, few of us have the alternative to inhabit that pace today. We need to go to work and need to take get-aways. A Greenhouse must have the capacity to care for itself to some degree. Some level of mechanization in a Greenhouse is attractive, even basic.

While considering what Greenhouse supplies you require a programmed watering framework ought to be at the highest priority on your rundown. Programmed watering frameworks work in various ways. The least complex is the inactive framework that depends on narrow tangling to draw water up from a repository. This is the least expensive framework. On the other hand you may utilize a funneled water framework that is controlled by a clock. These may nourish water to singular pots through an arrangement of drippers or spread water through a permeable pipe. Then again, you may settle on a moistening framework that waters the plants and showers fine water beads into the air.

Ventilation can be controlled consequently as well. There are electronic gadgets that will open a vent or the entryway of a Greenhouse when the temperature achieves a specific level and enable them to close when the temperature drops. A more complex choice is to introduce an electric fan that will remove air from the Greenhouse as the temperature rises and attract cooler air.

It is conceivable to alter the extractor fan utilized as a part of residential kitchens and restrooms or the kind that are found in cooker hoods. For the individuals who are not ready to do this a superior arrangement is to purchase an instant one. Your Greenhouse maker will offer fans that fit your model of Greenhouse. This is the most stylishly fulfilling arrangement.

Indeed, even with great watering and ventilation it will never be conceivable to accomplish so ideal a domain for your plants that you take out all irritations and ailments. Numerous cultivators select compound arrangements, yet others want to utilize natural techniques in their Greenhouse. A scope of predator bugs would now be able to be purchased that will manage most regular invasions in your Greenhouse. The most widely recognized plant sicknesses in the Greenhouse are identified with mold and organism. They are caused by a wrong harmony amongst temperature and moistness. On the off chance that you are endeavoring to develop plants together that require somewhat unique conditions it will be hard to keep away from a few issues. They can be dealt with productively with various fungicides which tests show to be protected. Be that as it may, you ought to dependably use as coordinated and store them far from youngsters.

Manure is an essential supply for fruitful Greenhouse developing. You should sustain the plants in your Greenhouse. They are developing at an enormous rate and regardless of whether they are planted straightforwardly in the earth require supplements.

Inorganic concoction manures function admirably and are accessible in details that suit specific sorts of plant and specific phases of development. You will require one compost for vegetative development and another for the blossoming and fruiting phase of a vegetation's.

An expanding number of Greenhouse workers lean toward natural bolsters for their plants. These are additionally broadly accessible in fluid and powder frame. They are exceptionally successful and create comes about that are similarly in the same class as the inorganic assortment. The decision is yours.

Some type of shading will be essential in many Greenhouses. The warmth of the sun can consume plants effortlessly. The best strategy is to cut uniquely made shade mesh to within the structure of the

Greenhouse. A similar arrangement of clasps you use for the shade mesh can be utilized to hold plant backings and air pocket wrap plastic in the winter.

Air pocket wrap is utilized to protect the Greenhouse. It is a discretionary additional. However, is greatly helpful and worth adding to your rundown of Greenhouse supplies. These recommendations cover a portion of the provisions you will requirement for your Greenhouse.

Chapter 15 - Supplies You'll Need For A More Productive Greenhouse

A Greenhouse is fundamentally an exceptionally basic thing. By methods for glass or plastic the sun's vitality is caught noticeable all around and soil with the goal that an encased space is warmed enabling plants to develop ideally. While the standard of the thing is essentially the villain, as it's been said, is in the detail.

To get the most out of your Greenhouse you will require a few supplies to make it a productive framework. Your point is make in a counterfeit situation the best developing conditions for plants that would not ordinarily flourish in northern scopes or at high elevation. Your plants require warmth and moistness, however they additionally require ventilation in light of the fact that without a decent wind current illness can come about.

You likewise need to get the most extreme number of plants into the moderately little space of your Greenhouse. Regardless of whether your point is foods grown from the ground for the kitchen or colorful blooms for the house or show seat you have to abuse your Greenhouse to the full degree of its potential. Else it just ends up plainly wasteful. A Greenhouse is an escalated framework.

Indeed, even you depend just on the sun's beams to warm your Greenhouse and don't have any type of supplementary warming you should consider a scope of gear. You will absolutely require a strategy for venting the Greenhouse. On a bright day a Greenhouse can turn out to be excessively hot and plants will endure. The most straightforward strategy is to exit there and open the entryway and a window. In any case, on the off chance that you are grinding away throughout the day or plan to take relaxes that isn't a tasteful arrangement. A programmed arrangement of ventilation for the Greenhouse is the appropriate response.

Programmed ventilation might be as basic as an electronic instrument that opens a window or a more intricate arrangement of fans. They are activated by an indoor regulator. You can begin with something fundamental and put resources into a more intricate framework as you build up your Greenhouse.

The same is valid for watering. I could exit to the Greenhouse with a watering can. Yet, would I like to do that four or five times each day in high season? Indeed, even the most excited producer may dither at that. No, a programmed watering framework is the appropriate response notwithstanding for a little Greenhouse. It can be very straightforward. An aloof framework utilizing fine tangling is modest and simple to keep up. At a more mind boggling level there are frameworks of dribble encourage funnels that convey water to the plants.

For all the year round growing a Greenhouse will positively require lighting. Lights will expand your developing season. There are various writes accessible for Greenhouses.

Conveying energy to the Greenhouse is a gifted activity. Get a circuit tester to introduce an open air control supply on the off chance that you don't as of now have one. The control frameworks themselves can be worked by an eager beginner. The parts are accessible at electronic specialist providers. The vast majority of us would presumably want to get them instant. They are a decent interest in the long haul since they will guarantee the best conditions for your plants and enable you to take a break.

You ought to likewise consider how you expect to develop your plants. Will the plants be in holders on seats or will they develop in the ground? Plants will develop cheerfully in the ground. However, in the event that you become a similar sort of plant a seemingly endless amount of time in a similar place there can be a development of malady. The customary response to this issue was to supplant the dirt in the Greenhouse every year. That more likely than not been extremely difficult work. A superior arrangement is to utilize a developing medium that can be supplanted yearly. Business preparing fertilizer is a perfect arrangement. These are typically light to deal with in light of the fact that they depend on peat or, shockingly better, coconut fiber or bark which are both feasible assets.

Seats, or Greenhouse organizing, is exceptionally helpful. Littler plants or seedlings can be set at a more elevated amount. They likewise give space to blending manure and repotting plants. On the off chance that the Greenhouse is to be utilized by somebody who has versatility issues then this turns out to be much more essential. A Greenhouse worker with restricted portability can get extraordinary joy from a Greenhouse in the event that it is arranged legitimately. Great access is essential for all plant specialists yet particularly so for those with versatility issues. A way of well laid clearing stones is basic for any Greenhouse.

Chapter 16 - What Every Gardener Needs To Know About Greenhouse Systems

The Greenhouse is a framework that endeavors to impersonate the characteristic framework in which plants develop in nature. We should intend to furnish the plants with water, light, warmth and supplements in the correct amounts and at the ideal time for the plants to flourish. That as well as we should plan to go one superior to nature and to tweak the Greenhouse framework to the point where it delivers the greatest yield for the base conceivable info.

The cash we spend on lighting, warming and watering our Greenhouse, sustaining the plants and treating them for bugs and maladies are the information sources. Our own particular time is another info and one that is regularly hard to find. Maybe a couple of us can invest as much energy as we might want in the Greenhouse.

Yields are the organic product, vegetables and blooms we gather from our Greenhouse. To some degree less quantifiable are the physical and mental advantages we get from working in the Greenhouse. Developing plants is a perceived method to battle pressure and sorrow.

We need to get the most yield we can from our Greenhouse. Boosting the product isn't contrary with the individual advantages since it is a joy to be in a Greenhouse that is functioning admirably.

It will think about the general Greenhouse framework as various interconnected subsystems. At the point when every one of these frameworks are working in agreement then the Greenhouse in general will work viably.

There are four essential subsystems: water, warmth, light and supplements. Give us a chance to take a gander at water.

Water is essential since it conveys supplements to the plants' underlying foundations. It is likewise essential to the leaves of the plant which require water to produce sustenance. The air of a Greenhouse should be wet and in addition the developing medium.

Straightforward manual watering is regularly insufficient when plants are in fast development. A programmed watering framework is the perfect method for giving the right measure of water. It can be determined to a clock contingent upon the developing conditions and the phase of the vegetation's.

The air in a Greenhouse can be kept wet by moistening. Programmed clouding frameworks are accessible. A supply of water will likewise help.

At the point when water is a costly info since it is metered then water ought to be gathered. A water barrel will store water from the top of a house and the Greenhouse. It would then be able to be drawn into the Greenhouse. Little and extremely dependable pumps are not accessible for this reason.

Warming is maybe the most costly info and should be controlled painstakingly by an indoor regulator. There is no reason for having a radiator on when it isn't important. You should painstakingly screen the temperature in the Greenhouse and outside.

Protection is smart thought amid the winter. This will enable you to lessen your warming bills.

Light is generally ample and for the most part free. It just turns into an issue in the winter when the day length is short and the sky overcast. Some manufactured lighting might be important in a Greenhouse.

The issue that light exhibits is that there can be excessively of it. Plants effectively consume in a Greenhouse and shading is indispensable in summer.

Supplements are indispensable for plant development. You should nourish the plants in the event that you need the most ideal outcomes. The most controlled arrangement of plant nourishment is the hydroponic framework in which plant establishes are suspended in a supplement rich arrangement. Plants can even develop on a sheet of glass if a thin film of supplements is continually ignored their underlying foundations. This functions admirably in a Greenhouse setting.

At the point when every one of these subsystems are functioning admirably at that point there will be little issue with plant illnesses and irritations. Where these happen it is important to take a gander at warm, light, water and supplement levels.

In principle it is conceivable in a sufficiently extensive Greenhouse to have a totally shut framework with no outer contributions aside from daylight. The plants themselves would deliver their own particular nourishment and keep up the right level of dampness. Reptiles and creepy crawlies would eat bugs. There would be no requirement for human mediation. That isn't feasible on a little scale and not attractive since we need to reap the products our Greenhouses deliver.

The human component is the most critical piece of your Greenhouse framework. You are its control framework. You should prepare yourself to do it well. As you pick up involvement and read about the subject you will turn out to be more capable and your Greenhouse will start to work as a proficient framework.

Chapter 17 - How Does A Greenhouse Work: The Benefits That Can Be Derived From Its Acts

When you see how your Greenhouse functions you will find that you can receive the most in return. You will feel certain to analysis and attempt new things. Your outcomes will be better and you will end up being the envy of your companions.

Regardless of whether you need to develop fancy subject or foods grown from the ground it pays to acquaint yourself with the way a Greenhouse works. Investing a little energy in fundamental standards will pay off at last.

A Greenhouse is the primary, most straightforward presumably still the best sun based gadget known to mankind. We hear such a great amount about sun based boards and other cutting edge contraptions, you may even have one of those helpful sunlight based controlled gadgets to charge batteries, however the Greenhouse is from numerous points of view a sun oriented fueled gadget as well.

The Greenhouse varies from other later sun based fueled gadgets in that it has been around for so long it has been refined to the point that it works extremely well. It does its activity flawlessly.

That activity is warming. A Greenhouse utilizes the sun's beams to warm up the developing medium and air in an encased space. It will do that with no assistance from us or any additional items.

In principle it is conceivable to make a Greenhouse that was totally independent that could exist with no human mediation once the framework was running. The plants inside it would make their own particular environment by giving out oxygen and taking in carbon dioxide. Such a Greenhouse would be a model of the whole planet.

It would need to be a major Greenhouse, surely greater than you would need in your terrace, and remains the stuff of sci-fi right now. We have not exactly accomplished "quiet running" yet. Be that as it may, thinking about a Greenhouse along these lines encourages you to comprehend that you are managing a living framework.

You need to assume a dynamic part to keep the living framework in your Greenhouse in adjust. You are the control arrangement of the Greenhouse.

The Greenhouse will carry out its activity of warming as long the sun sparkles with no assistance from you. However, once you place plants in there then the issues start. The plants won't simply take care of themselves.

A Greenhouse is too little and the plants are normally excessively thick for them, making it impossible to act naturally adequate. You should give them water and you should manage the air.

When I say manage the climate what I am discussing is mugginess. Stickiness is the measure of water held noticeable all around. The measure of water that air will hold relies upon the temperature of the air. Air at 70 degrees will hold twice as much water as air at 55 degrees.

At the point when the temperature of the Greenhouse starts to fall the water drops out of the air. This is known as the dew point. On the off chance that plants are subjected to this for a long stretch they are at risk to experience the ill effects of different types of spoil, form, parasite and buildup.

This is a characteristic piece of the plant's lifecycle however not bravo in the event that we need great quality products from our Greenhouse. You can treat the plants with chemicals. There are a lot of fungicides accessible available. Be that as it may, it is smarter to maintain a strategic distance from the issue quite far by ventilating the Greenhouse.

The measure of ventilation will rely upon the temperature. You require more ventilation at bring down temperatures. Open the entryway and a window, or utilize an extractor fan. In any case you do it get that air moving.

Dampness is identified with watering. On the off chance that you apply excessively water to the developing medium or water accumulates on ways and organizing in the Greenhouse you will have issues with stickiness. Expect to have well depleting ways and surfaces in your Greenhouse.

It is conceivable to quantify the moistness of your Greenhouse with a sling psychrometer. This is a gadget comprising of two thermometers. One thermometer has a wick that can be wet. You turn the entire gadget for a couple of minutes at that point take a perusing from every thermometer. Subtract the perusing of the wet one from the dry one and contrast the perusing with the diagram gave. That will give you the relative dampness.

This basic gadget will empower you to direct your watering and ventilation administration in the Greenhouse. When you get those correct you will take out a considerable measure of the issues basic to Greenhouses. Your Greenhouse framework will function admirably.

Chapter 18 - The Purposes Of Hydroponics Greenhouses

Hydroponics has been honed for quite a long time. It is imagined that the Hanging Gardens of Babylon were a hydroponic framework. In its cutting edge shape it was produced amid the Second World War. US Air compel staff utilized hydroponics to develop crops at army installations in the Middle East and Pacific.

With the approach of new plastic materials and new developing mediums hydroponics has turned into a pragmatic recommendation for the novice. It is as of now broadly utilized as a part of business Greenhouses.

The benefit of hydroponics is that it enables the cultivator to control the supplements that are nourished to the plant with incredible exactitude. Nothing is squandered and plants get precisely the supplements they require at each phase in their life cycle.

There are various techniques that are suited to the novice and can be set up in a residential Greenhouse. The most well-known is presumably the surge and deplete strategy yet the thin supplement film technique is picking up in fame. Both are in a perfect world suited to the Greenhouse.

An elective technique is profound water hydroponics. This is less appropriate for the Greenhouse. Be that as it may, it might have applications when utilized as a part of conjunction with angle keeping. The waste discharged by the fish demonstrations a wellspring of supplements for plants. This kind of hydroponics or aquaculture is maybe excessively concentrated for most specialists however worth remembering.

For most Greenhouses a surge and deplete framework or a thin supplement film technique will function admirably and they are not hard to construct. The essential supplies are accessible from authority retailers the greater part of whom have sites. They will be satisfied to prompt a beginner about the best hardware for their Greenhouse.

A significant number of the provisions that you will need can be sourced from your nearby equipment retailer. Square segment water guttering, plastic pipes and water tanks are sufficiently simple to discover. A lot of an average Greenhouse hydroponic framework can be made by a beginner.

The nourishment and deplete framework includes flooding water into a plant holder and afterward giving it a chance to deplete out once more. It is as straightforward as that. Your Greenhouse should be furnished with a store for water, funnels to transport it and a pump to circle the water around the framework.

You require a plate or other holder with an outlet for the water. The holder ought to be loaded with a developing medium, for example, perlite, coconut fiber, rockwool or mud stones. Rockwool is most regularly utilized as a part of business Greenhouses.

The thin supplement film functions admirably in the Greenhouse. It just requires a water verification surface. Indeed, even a sheet of glass will do. An unfaltering stream of water is run continually finished the roots.

Uncommon hydroponic supplements are accessible. They are intended for general use, for particular products, or for specific phases of development. These must be added to the store in the amount indicated by the producer. Every one of the plants in your Greenhouse can be bolstered from a typical source through an arrangement of channels prompting and from the repository.

A straightforward hydroponic framework may comprise of a progression of water drains running down either side of a rectangular Greenhouse with a repository toward one side. To take advantage of the space in your Greenhouse you can orchestrate the drains in levels. A bigger Greenhouse may have canals organized over the width of the Greenhouse.

A more created framework in a huge Greenhouse could put the drains on rollers with the goal that they be moved. A productive arrangement of sowing toward one side and gathering at the other can be accomplished utilizing this framework.

In a roundabout Greenhouse an arrangement of plate may be more proficient. In the event that they all slant down to a focal repository the requirement for funneling will be limited. The store can be secured with decking so you can remain on it tend the plants.

Hydroponic frameworks work best if the water is warmed to around 55 degrees. This temperature is will be come to in many Greenhouses amid the mid year. Be that as it may, in the winter you may need to warm the supply when you warm whatever is left of the Greenhouse.

Hydroponic frameworks can be utilized out of entryways, yet they truly make their mark in the Greenhouse. The upside of hydroponics in the Greenhouse is that is enables you to practice finish control over your Greenhouse. Not exclusively is the temperature, watering and air of the Greenhouse under your hands however so is the correct level of supplements encouraged to the plants.

Chapter 19 - What You Get From 'Lean-To' Greenhouses

A shelter Greenhouse is maybe the least complex and most flexible type of Greenhouse accessible. It fits home development and can be fitted into a restricted space. Its trademark highlight is that is makes utilization of a current structure. It may be worked against the mass of a house, carport or a limit divider.

A shelter Greenhouse may be a basic brief structure made of plastic sheeting or it may be a detailed perpetual structure that could be stately with the name "center". Whichever way it is a shelter Greenhouse. It contrasts from different kinds of Greenhouse in not being a detached structure.

The shelter Greenhouse has a notoriety for being a make-move structure, however there is no motivation behind why it ought to be. The exemplary vine place of the nineteenth century was regularly a shelter structure work along the mass of the vegetable garden of an English stately home.

Those of us with littler spending plans can in any case exploit the advantages offered by a shelter Greenhouse. The primary preferred standpoint that is one of a kind to the shelter Greenhouse is that the divider against which it is assembled goes about as a warmth store. A south-bound divider that gets the sun's beams for the duration of the day will give out warmth throughout the night. The divider goes about as a sort of capacity warmer. Proprietors of different sorts of Greenhouse attempt a wide range of catalysts to accomplish a similar sort of warm properties that a shelter Greenhouse has normally.

A shelter Greenhouse has greener qualifications since it holds warm along these lines. Less supplementary warming is required for a shelter Greenhouse than a detached structure. It might likewise offer advantages to the house that it is worked against. The shelter Greenhouse can go about as a wellspring of sun oriented warming for the house.

The other primary favorable position of the shelter Greenhouse is its tallness. Its stature is restricted by the tallness of the divider against which the shelter Greenhouse is manufactured, yet even so there is less squandered space than in numerous different sorts of Greenhouse. A shelter Greenhouse offers more usable space than the well-known vault formed Greenhouse.

Therefore, the shelter Greenhouse is the perfect decision where space is constrained. The shelter Greenhouse can even be developed on a little porch or gallery. Indeed, even a rooftop garden could oblige a shelter Greenhouse. Nobody require be rejected from Greenhouse planting. A similarly little space can yield amazing outcomes with a shelter Greenhouse.

Now and again it is conceivable to fill the while of a shelter Greenhouse with plants without holding any space for an entrance way. The Greenhouse worker can get to the plants from outside the shelter Greenhouse if the sides can be opened by methods for sliding boards.

As in some other Greenhouse the shelter Greenhouse needs satisfactory arrangement for warming, ventilation and watering. You will most likely need to mechanize these frameworks to some degree. It might be conceivable to accomplish this all the more effectively in a shelter Greenhouse on account of its vicinity to the house. With a shelter Greenhouse it is less demanding to keep running in a supply of water and power than it would be at some separation from the house.

Are there any weaknesses to the shelter Greenhouse? Indeed, however very few and they can be overcome.

While building a shelter Greenhouse guarantee that the a decent waterproof seal is accomplished with the divider. This is especially basic on the off chance that it is work against a house divider. Blazing must be utilized as a part of this specific situation. Else you will get water leakage and the divider will progress toward becoming stained with form. In the event that you are working against a garden divider this isn't such a noteworthy issue.

It might be important to check whether your proposed shelter Greenhouse negates any building controls. The measure of structure or the materials might be constrained. so discover before you begin and commit an expensive error.

So unattached structure or shelter Greenhouse the decision is yours. Be that as it may, there are numerous favorable circumstances to the shelter Greenhouse. The shelter Greenhouse offers the best utilization of room and great warm properties. Try not to give the old picture of the shelter Greenhouse put you a chance to off. It is conceivable to build up a stylishly satisfying plan for the shelter Greenhouse.

Chapter 20 - Greenhouses Ideal For Small Areas

Numerous individuals might want to develop plants however don't have much space. You may just have a gallery or a minor yard. The littler the space you have the more sense it makes to utilization of Greenhouse since it empower you to benefit as much as possible from that space all the year round.

A modest territory can create an astonishing measure of plants on the off chance that it is drawn closer in the correct way. You may not end up plainly independent in products of the soil but rather you will have the capacity to grow a supply of new servings of mixed greens and herbs or blooms for the home from even a little Greenhouse.

The Greenhouse is an escalated arrangement of developing and that is the thing that you require in the event that you have just a little space accessible. Regardless of whether you have a lot of land you might need to consider a smaller than normal Greenhouse beside kitchen entryway with the goal that you can get a modest bunch of herbs or serving of mixed greens as you get ready dinner. You may as of now have a vast Greenhouse however may need a little Greenhouse for some additional plants.

A little Greenhouse can be exceptionally straightforward and shoddy. It might be close to a tubular steel structure secured with a plastic tent. They normally have a zip latch at the front with the goal that you can open the shelter.

Greenhouses of this write are accessible in a scope of sizes. They can be purchased for under $100.

They as a rule have a few retires that enable you to grow various little plants in pots or plate. On the off chance that you put it beside a south-bound divider every rack of a little Greenhouse like this will get enough life to enable the plants to flourish.

On the off chance that you need to develop tall plants in your Greenhouse you can take the racks out. Yet, there are numerous elective assortments of plants that have a little shape. Pick shrub or following tomatoes, for instance. They will fit cheerfully on the racks of your little Greenhouse.

It might be a smart thought to settle your Greenhouse to the divider on the off chance that you live in breezy region or on the off chance that you have youngsters or a canine. They can without much of a stretch be thumped over and your valuable plants with them. On the off chance that you need to utilize your smaller than expected Greenhouse on an overhang ensure that you secure it well.

Similarly as in bigger Greenhouses it is conceivable to have programmed watering frameworks for little Greenhouses. You could orchestrate a trickle bolster water system framework that watered all your hanging containers and grower and additionally your scaled down Greenhouse.

On the off chance that all you need to do is water the smaller than normal Greenhouse then an inactive watering framework utilizing slender tangling might be sufficient. You will require a store of water at the base. Put dark plastic on every rack and cover it with narrow tangling. Splash the entire thing before you begin at that point put the plant pots on the racks.

You can even make a little Greenhouse into a hydroponic framework by putting plate on every rack and enabling water to rundown through each of them thusly. You would require a little pump. They cost under $30. Simply penetrate a gap in one end of every plate and tilt it marginally to enable the water to deplete. Fix a pipe at the edge of your smaller than normal Greenhouse to take water to the best and turn on the pump.

One of the immense points of interest of smaller than normal Greenhouses is that plants can be raised up off the beaten path of slugs. An entire plate of basil seedlings can be eaten by slugs before you have out of bed toward the beginning of the day. In the event that you wrap some copper tape around the legs of your Greenhouse the slugs will dither to ascend and get your new plants.

Plastic secured little Greenhouses have a tendency to be less enduring that huge Greenhouses that are all the more powerfully developed. In any case, you can get numerous times of utilization out of them. You ought to be set up to change the covering on your smaller than usual Greenhouse consistently. The system will last any longer and can be reused over and over.

On the off chance that you have an exceptionally minor space the entire smaller than expected Greenhouse can be brought down in the mid year and put away until the winter. Another option is to remove the cover and utilize the racks to show your plants. Your smaller than usual Greenhouse will give a mass of green on your overhang or porch. Take some house plants out for an airing put them on the racks of your smaller than expected Greenhouse. What might some way or another look rather utilitarian will start to look very enriching.

Chapter 21 - Considering Buying A Greenhouse?

Because of the consistently developing interest of nourishment caused by a quick increment in human populace, agrarian assets are getting over extended. On account of land, agriculturists have been enticed to expand profitability by abuse of manures and disposal of vermin by utilizing chemicals. Accordingly, the environmental adjust has been bothered making a few issues ranchers. Moreover, extraordinary climate designs because of a worldwide temperature alteration have likewise raised the apparition of loss of efficiency. Looked with these issues, an agriculturist may be enticed settle on the troublesome decision of auctioning off the land held by the family for a considerable length of time.

The Arrangement

Researchers and horticulture specialists advocate that agriculturists make utilize Greenhouses. Fundamentally, a Greenhouse is an encased structure where yields can be developed in a controlled domain. Inside a Greenhouse, conditions required for perfect development of yields can be given, for example, water, daylight, supplements controlled temperature and nonattendance of vermin. As of now Greenhouses have been effectively used to develop blooms and tests have now demonstrated that these can be utilized to build edit profitability up to 10 times. Greenhouses can be especially valuable in expanding the profitability of products of the soil.

Development

A Greenhouses can be developed in different shapes and sizes, contingent on the climatic states of the region where it is to be introduced. In such manner, different materials can be utilized as a part of its development. A region impacted by solid climate examples, for example, winds and tempests would require a metallic structure for the Greenhouse to survive. The framing of the Greenhouse in these conditions would preferably require a smash evidence material, for example, plastic or Plexiglas, as against basic glass. Correspondingly, a Greenhouse intended to be introduced in a saline situation, presented to a solid ocean breeze for instance, would require a rust verification metallic structure to guarantee a sensible administration life. Then again, a zone encountering delicate breezes and light rain could just be made as a polythene tent extended over wood.

Handiness

Greenhouses are particularly helpful amid winters. Snow, ice and hails are known to make impressive harm crops. A Greenhouse could be provided with warmers or protection to avert ice amid evening. Besides, amid daytime, a Greenhouse demonstrations to trap warm from the sun inside its walled in area henceforth the expression "Greenhouse impact" used to depict a dangerous atmospheric devation. The "Greenhouse impact" in the walled in area would give high temperature that is expected to save plants amid winters.

Regarding the financial viewpoints related with its establishment, a Greenhouse is probably going to pay for its establishment and support costs by expanding the homesteads gainfulness complex. In such manner, an agriculturist must be cautious in order to consider the neighborhood climatic conditions previously settling on the sort of Greenhouse to be introduced. It would be exceptionally prescribed to consider a specialist sentiment before choosing to get one.

Like every single other field of business, horticulture additionally requires development and the utilization of research to expand its productivity. In this unique situation, the field of horticulture likewise accompanies its dangers like different undertakings. For this situation, dangers appear as maladies, irritations and extraordinary climate designs. A Greenhouse serves to lessen these dangers with a specific end goal to encourage increment in productivity. A painstakingly chose Greenhouse would in this manner prompt an expansion in edit creation that would at last contribute towards the monetary elevate of the rancher.

Chapter 22 - Rules For Constructing Your Commercial Greenhouse

The gainfulness of a Greenhouse incredibly relies upon different elements that identify with the plants that are being developed inside it. In such manner, mind must be taken in order to pick the correct sort of development for the fitting yields. Climatic states of the region of establishment and its geology should likewise be given due thought.

Kinds of Greenhouses

There are different kinds of developments accessible for Greenhouses. These incorporate segregated Greenhouses which stand free of each other. Access can however be given by methods for a passageway connecting a few confined Greenhouses to each other. One case of such Greenhouses is the Quonset compose. These are the most widely recognized write that are built utilizing curved rafters and have strong dividers for extra help. These are thought to be proper for generally edits.

Another sort of Greenhouse is usually known as an edge Greenhouse. These are joined through the eave by a common drain, subsequently allowing expanded efficiency. Edge compose Greenhouses can be either bended or gabled. While gabled Greenhouses are more appropriate to be secured by significant sheets, bended Greenhouses are more suited for lighter covering materials, for example, polytene.

Setting up a Greenhouse

While intending to setup a Greenhouse, a few components ought to be considered. There must be legitimate access to business sectors, utilities and transport offices. In addition, prospects of future extension should likewise be considered.

Different components that must be considered before setting up a Greenhouse incorporate the harvests one is keen on developing, the developing period of that yield, developing period. Besides the developing medium, for example, water, soil, sand, compost should likewise be characterized. What's more, the cultivating strategies, for example, flooring, developing pots, seats and so on must likewise be considered. Last however

not the slightest come the money related perspectives that incorporate advertising, efficiency and the venture required.

The Business angles

When setting up a Greenhouse, there are different business angles that must not be neglected. In this regard, the territory used to set up a Greenhouse must associate with two sections of land for it to be economically suitable. This requires space for vehicular movement related with the utilized labor and in addition transport of the item. Besides, the Greenhouse must be situated in a region where it is allowed by government directions. Moreover, there must be street access to the site to guarantee effective conveyance of the reap to the market and smooth supply of seeds, manures and upkeep gear.

It is likewise critical that the site is found far from modern contamination, since the item is implied for human utilization. Modern effluents are probably going to bring toxic chemicals into the item that would have antagonistic impact on people groups' wellbeing. Since a Greenhouse basically traps warm from daylight, the site must get sufficient measure of daylight, particularly amid winter season.

As far as utilities, the site must approach water and power. Water is basic for the development of all plant shapes. Notwithstanding, the supply must be appropriately tried for contaminations that could hurt the yield. Power, then again is basic for keeping up the controlled condition inside the Greenhouse, and in addition to run the hardware expected to develop and gather the plant.

Ultimately, similar to all different business enterprises, space for future development must be accessible for this situation. In such manner, watchful arranging is the way to progress. Plan well and your business will thrive.

Chapter 23 - 5 Essentials For A Commercial Greenhouse

The interest for business Greenhouses has encountered a fast increment in the United States. The province of Georgia alone records for more than 11 million square feet zone secured with business Greenhouses. This grow can well be credited to ascend in the interest for normal nourishment items. While business Greenhouses do give a fantastic chance to ranchers for expanding the efficiency and gainfulness of their possessions, it must be borne as a top priority that arrangement of fundamental gear is basic for understanding these advantages. In such manner, a business Greenhouse must be outfitted with the accompanying basics:

1. Business Greenhouse warmers

Amid the winter season, now and again the arrangement of a warmth source inside a Greenhouse might be basic to guarantee edit survival. Indeed, even one cool day could fundamentally decrease the profitability plants. Since a Greenhouse typically traps warm from daylight inside its walled in area, a radiator may prove to be useful amid overcast days. It is in this manner prudent to introduce a solid business radiator in a business Greenhouse. The cost of running the radiator amid sunless days would be exceeded by the expansion in efficiency.

2. A strong Greenhouse organizing

A business Greenhouse will probably witness heavier burdens being places and transported inside its compound than non-business Greenhouses. These incorporate more noteworthy heaps of collect, substantial pots and seats that are utilized to develop the plants. It is in this manner imperative that the Greenhouse arranging used to move these overwhelming burdens inside the Greenhouse is substantial obligation and solid.

3. Seed plate rack

Most business crops grow from seeds and keeping in mind the end goal to develop greatest number of yields consistently, one must guarantee the arrangement of seed plate retires or racks. Since space is valuable inside a Greenhouse, these racks or retires could save room that could be utilized to develop extra products. Along these lines profitability can be additionally expanded.

4. Watering hardware

Business Greenhouses are by definition considerably more broad that their non-business partners. It is along these lines tedious and excessively requesting, making it impossible to water the products physically. Besides, monitoring the plants that have been watered is additionally a significant test if manual watering is attempted. A cutting edge and proficient plant watering framework is in this way basic in a business Greenhouse to guarantee ideal profitability amid reap.

5. Thermometers

The fundamental reason for a Greenhouse is to furnish plants with ideal surrounding conditions that would prompt most extreme efficiency. Of these, temperature is generally basic. It is accordingly not fitting to depend exclusively on human senses to control this imperative parameter. In this specific situation, it is imperative to take note of that even slight varieties in temperature could enormously influence the measure of collect that you procure. In addition, its is excessively tedious for a man, making it impossible to screen the temperature inside the Greenhouse round the clock. The arrangement of thermometers should along these lines be guaranteed in a business Greenhouse. In such manner, a programmed temperature control instrument which does not require a human administrator would be ideal.

The arrangement of these basic contraptions would significantly expand the profitability of a Greenhouse. That would thusly help benefits that are the soul behind any business endeavor. Besides, effective plug ranchers can appropriately take pride in the commitment they make for the advantage of the group, nature and even the entire of mankind.

Chapter 24 - Business Greenhouse Kits

Business Greenhouse packs could turn out to be very helpful for new participants into this undertaking. It furnishes the financial specialist with the correct sort of apparatuses and gear expected to embrace this business. With such a pack, one can instantly set out upon a business Greenhouse venture.

Focuses to be considered before acquiring business Greenhouse packs

Before really making the buy, you should design well, get your course straight and be aware of your objectives. It is along these lines firmly prompted that you do appropriate pre-buy arranging and investigate, and consider over the different advantages and disadvantages related with your task. In this unique situation, it would be beneficial that you accumulate greatest data about Greenhouses.

Furthermore, before going for the buy, one must settle on the measure of Greenhouse That would be set up. This relies on the span of one's holding and the idea of the product and the sum venture that is accessible. For sure, a larger than average Greenhouse will be more costly to keep up on the off chance that you don't have enough funding to completely populate it with plants. Purge spaces may at present be spending your assets and could add to your overheads.

Another critical point that must be considered before procuring your pack is the kind of plants that would top off your Greenhouse. Since, a business wander is constantly esteemed as far as productivity, it is fitting to develop crops that are sought after. Once the kind of product is chosen, the parameters related with the Greenhouse, for example, its size, the medium of development and the condition that will be kept up inside can be resolved. In case your products require more space, your pack ought to incorporate space sparing hardware, for example, racks. On the off chance that the plants are touchy to temperature variety, it is a smart thought to get a pack that incorporates delicate thermometers and temperature control contraptions, for example, radiators and indoor regulator-based systems to manage temperature.

There are different kinds of business Greenhouse that are accessible. Picking the best plan that is perfect for your business is additionally an imperative choice you have to make before you really go ahead to buy a business Greenhouse pack. In such manner, you should be aware of your necessities it terms of the geography and atmosphere of your site. Going for a costly outline that may not be required in your general vicinity could pointlessly deplete your financial plan. The sum squandered consequently could on the other hand be utilized to purchase other helpful types of gear that could build the measure of your reap.

Commentary: When purchasing a business Greenhouse pack, you should be clear about your necessities keeping in mind the end goal to purchase the correct stuff to begin your business.

Chapter 25 - Free Greenhouse Plan For You

"Plant darlings", that is individuals who have an enthusiasm towards keeping up gardens in their terraces and tending to plants would normally be keen on raising a Greenhouse. In this specific situation, a Greenhouse ought to be all around planned and developed with the goal that it is anything but difficult to keep up and does not offer inconvenience to its proprietor.

With a specific end goal to guarantee the prosperity of plants developed inside it, a Greenhouse must have a proficient watering and moistening proliferation framework. Such a framework should screen and keep up the level of dampness inside the Greenhouse. Water is a valuable normal asset that ought to be saved. Keep in mind, one of the advantages credited to Greenhouses is that they are useful for nature. Your Greenhouse must have the capacity to make utilization of water, rather than depending exclusively in water being provided as an utility. An arrangement of canals and downspouts should hence be set up to water the product utilizing regular water. It would likewise be a smart thought to have an arrangement for putting away water for future use.

The Greenhouse must be given power or flammable gas (whichever is advantageous) to fuel radiators that would be valuable in keeping up ideal temperature amid icy spells. It might be considered that plants use light to develop by the procedure of photosynthesis. Lights may in this manner be introduced inside with the goal that plant development isn't hindered because of absence of daylight.

Over the web, one can discover numerous sites that offer rules on the best way to setup a Greenhouse. These may incorporate plans that would offer assistance in arranging the Greenhouses with water supply frameworks. Others may contain directions on the most proficient method to get to know and apply the right now mainstream procedures of hydroponics cultivating. A few sites likewise offer free gets ready for setting up a detached Greenhouse.

Building your Greenhouse

For amateurs, The accompanying rules would be useful in setting up a little Greenhouse utilizing ease, simple to gain materials:

For setting up your Greenhouse you would require things including around one and about six press cuts, a move of channel tape, 3 moves overwhelming obligation 3M clear tape, 6 mm clear plastic, 18 tightening tie downs, 4 to 8 T posts, 10 x 20 Universal covering and discretionary lights and radiators. While amassing the Greenhouse, it is advantageous to look for help of 2-3 people who might be your companions or relatives. These individuals could give you some assistance in setting up the system and holding things in position while you introduce them. While making associations, pipe tape must be utilized appropriately in order to guarantee that association focuses are watertight.

Initially, you should associate the 18 attach downs to interface with the upper piece of the casing. You may utilize four T presents on help the four corners of the structure. When this is done, put an additional T-post inside the casing and penetrate it no less than 12" into the ground. In the following stage, utilize the plastic sheet to cover your Greenhouse. Extend the sheet over structure that has just been introduced, utilizing a stepping stool. Utilize some overwhelming articles like stones, heaps of rock or even vases with the goal that the sheet remains immovably on the ground and does not overwhelm by wing.

Congrats! You have influenced your own special low-to cost Greenhouse

Chapter 26 - Greenhouse Accessories And Their Utility

A Greenhouse is intended to hatch plants inside its fenced in area keeping in mind the end goal to shield them from climatic furthest points regarding temperature, mugginess and wind. Its capacities based on the "Greenhouse impact" whereby daylight and infra red radiation from the sun enters the Greenhouse. Upon reflection, these beams are caught inside Greenhouse, in this way adding to an ascent in temperature inside it. It merits watching the way that in this basic setup, the wellspring of warmth is fundamentally the sun. In any case, amid eras when daylight isn't accessible because of shady skies, radiators might be utilized to keep up ideal temperature. On the other hand, amid hot spells, temperature might be brought around methods for fog sprayers or fumes fans.

Since upkeep of reasonable conditions inside its degree is the essential capacity of a Greenhouse, certain contraptions are regarded fundamental for its legitimate misuse. The utilization of these devices is important to keep up the conditions inside the Greenhouse at the level fundamental for plant survival. These embellishments include:

Thermometers

Temperature is the most basic parameter that must be directed inside a Greenhouse to guarantee a solid manor. Extremely chilly temperatures are probably going to stunt the development of plants and in specific cases may prompt their pulverization. Hot conditions, then again, could "wear out" the plants. By methods for thermometers, the temperature inside a Greenhouse can without much of a stretch be observed and medicinal measures can be arranged at whatever point it goes basic.

Indoor regulators

Indoor regulators are programmed gadgets that can distinguish temperature changes, as well as control it. These could be as a basic robotized window that opens to the environment on the off chance that temperature levels go extraordinary. Other more modern indoor regulators can likewise be introduced to keep up temperature levels in a Greenhouse.

Humidistat

Support of moistness inside a Greenhouse is likewise essential for the prosperity of plants. AS on account of an indoor regulator which manages temperature, humidistats are gadgets that keep up dampness levels to ideal inside a Greenhouse. These gadgets are especially valuable amid hot conditions, when dampness substance accessible to plants are exhausted by climatic warmth making them dry out and consume. When plants get "scorched", they basically lose chlorophyll - the substance that gives them their green shading. Chlorophyll is fundamental for the procedure of photosynthesis by which plants make supplements.

Lighting frameworks

Plants make their sustenance utilizing supplements from the dirt, dampness and daylight. This procedure is known as photosynthesis whereby vitality from daylight is

used to control the substance response that produces starches within the sight of chlorophyll. Sugars are the essential units that make up our sustenance.

Amid certain climatic spells when daylight isn't accessible for drawn out eras, contraptions known as develop lights can give a valuable option,

in this way avoiding degeneration of yields.

Light meters

Like every other response, a lot of light might be unsafe for plant wellbeing. This plan of action, similar to temperature and water, should likewise be given at ideal level. Light meters can help with identifying the measure of light plants are being presented to inside the Greenhouse. Along these lines, light can be directed by utilizing basic light channels like off-white glass.

While intending to introduce the previously mentioned frill, one must be aware of the nearby conditions winning in the territory where the Greenhouse is arranged. It is principally these conditions which direct the kind of accomplice to be introduced in the Greenhouse.

Chapter 27 - Greenhouse Designs

Given the tremendous number of advantages related with them, regarding plant wellbeing, condition and additionally gainfulness, Greenhouses are positively justified regardless of the venture made to introduce and look after them. This is valid for both novice plant specialists and also prepared horticulturalists. For specialists, the measure of euphoria one gets from seeing their plants blossom is sufficient to reimburse their venture. For proficient speculators, the monetary benefits related with a Greenhouse are copious. Notwithstanding, since obtaining your Greenhouse can be costly inferable from benefits and commissions related with those engaged with its assembling, transportation, promoting and deal, it is critical that you pick the plan that is most appropriate to your requirements, and in addition installable in at your site.

Kinds of Greenhouses

Fundamentally Greenhouses can be characterized into two general classifications: the appended compose and the detached kind.

Detached Greenhouses

Greenhouses that fall in this classification can be recognized for the other sort in that these are unsupported structures raised free of your home. Thus, these kind of Greenhouses can be arranged in order to get greatest introduction to daylight. Be that as it may, since it is separate from the house, the Greenhouse should be outfitted with lighting and ought to be provided with power and water. This classification can additionally be subdivided into two classes:

1. Juliana Greenhouse

Structures adjusting to this class are most appropriate for constrained spaces. This outline is likewise suited for newbies. Since neither silicone nor cuts are utilized as a part of its development, it makes the impression of a crisp plan.

2. Hideaway outline

This outline is set apart by its openness. It can likewise fill in as an escape from ordinary schedules where you can unwind alone. Since this plan utilizes transparent polycarbonate material. This material comes covered with a bright covering. Bright beams from daylight are especially unsafe to people as they can cause sunburns and skin growth. These beams are additionally not useful for plants. Since this sort of Greenhouse is planned with the end goal that it channels the cancer-causing ultra-violet light, the subsequent delicate scattered light is useful for your wellbeing and your plants. Along these lines you can likewise relax in sun without worrying about sunburns and skin disease. The nonattendance of the unsafe UV beams likewise implies that you don't need to intermittently apply sun pieces to secure yourself.

Joined Greenhouses

Joined Greenhouses are not detached structures, but rather depend on your home for their auxiliary help and honesty. Cases of this write incorporate the even-traverse compose and the window mounted compose. The previous outline can be named a full-measure show, with the exception of that one of its side is joined to the house for help. It gives more space to plants that a window-mounted outline. The window mounted outline, then again, is affixed in a window. This write is exceptionally temperate and requires slightest measure of room.

While costs change contingent upon the outline you pick, it is vital that you pick the correct plan that suites your requirements. Indeed, even an improper outline accompanies its cost and on the off chance that you are not happy with it, it would be an exercise in futility and additionally cash.

Chapter 28 - Treating Greenhouse Plants

Green plants are portrayed by their capacity to make their own particular sustenance by a procedure called photosynthesis. By this procedure, plants join carbon dioxide from air, and water and supplements from the dirt, similar to nitrates, phosphates and sulfates, to make nourishment substances. Daylight is utilized as the wellspring of vitality to control this procedure. While the easiest sustenance item is as sugars, which just framed from carbon dioxide and water, higher natural mixes like proteins and minerals that are basic parts of development require supplements from soil. Manures go about as a hotspot for these supplements. Composts additionally add porosity to the dirt, which is vital as in it builds the dirt's ability to hold water and air without suffocating the plant.

Composts could be in strong frame or fluid. The sort of compost required for your yields relies upon the kind of plants you have planted. This is because of the way that each plant has its own requirements for various substances that are basic for its development. Amid seasons that animate fast development of specific plants, as in the spring season, these plants must be prepared once every month or two. Plants that experience nonstop development consistently, then again, require an unfaltering supply of manures.

What are composts?

As specified some time recently, manures are substances that go about as wellsprings of basic supplements like nitrogen, press, phosphorous, sulfur and different components. Nitrogen is the most critical of these since it is utilized to make proteins. Proteins are one of the principle nutrition types alongside fats and sugars. Not at all like fats and sugars, which just contain carbon, hydrogen and oxygen, proteins contain nitrogen notwithstanding these three components. Proteins are viewed as building pieces of life. Keeping in mind the end goal to supply this fundamental component, manures are rich in nitrogen, which is as a rule around half. Peat-like composts, which contain nitrate-F are ideal for use in Greenhouses by specialists. Greenhouse Gradecalcium nitrate in could likewise be connected for huge scale developing.

Utilization of composts

Composts are typically suggested for specific kinds of plants. Before applying to your plants, you should deliberately read the name and look for a specialist feeling with respect to their utilization. Providers and lists can likewise give you helpful data with respect to their utilization. The supposition of a qualified plant growth specialist of a plant pathologist would positively be more valuable.

It is critical that manures supply an adjusted eating regimen to plants for their development. Dissolvable or fluid composts convey speedier outcomes as contrasted and strong ones. Their application is as straightforward as watering plants. More grounded than prescribed measurements are however not suggested as these would harm their underlying foundations and could in the long run execute them. It is along these lines a smart thought to really apply weaker than prescribed measurements to plants. This ca effortlessly be finished by weakening the treated with water.

Applying a blend of various evaluations of composts is likewise a decent strategy in order to satisfy the requirements of the kind of plants that are being developed. This will likewise guarantee that the plant is provided with the particular chemicals it needs at the different phases of its life.

Greenhouse plants require your consideration. Checking them every day for their prosperity is both fulfilling and give you a feeling of achievement. Make sure that they are free from malady and bugs and thrive. Their survival is your prosperity.

Chapter 29 - Treatment Of Greenhouse Crops

Greenhouses are utilized to furnish crops with a good domain that would trigger their solid development. While the arrangement of ideal temperature, moistness level and water supply are essential worries in a Greenhouse, the supply of supplements is likewise an imperative viewpoint that must be provided food for in a Greenhouse.

What are manures?

Plants can produce their own sustenance by a procedure called photosynthesis. By this procedure, plants join carbon dioxide from air, and water and supplements from the dirt, similar to nitrates, phosphates and sulfates, to make nourishment substances. Daylight is utilized as the wellspring of vitality to control this procedure. While the least complex nourishment item is as sugars, which just framed from carbon dioxide and water, higher natural mixes like proteins and minerals that are fundamental parts of development require supplements from soil. Composts go about as a hotspot for these supplements. Composts likewise add porosity to the dirt, which is essential as in it expands the dirt's ability to hold water and air without suffocating the plant. In open nature, plants get a consistent supply of supplements through rotting natural issue and creature squander as excrement. In any case, since a Greenhouse is separated from the open condition, the supply of supplements is basic. Manures are basically substances that go about as wellsprings of basic supplements like nitrogen, press, phosphorous, sulfur and different components. Nitrogen is the most essential of these since it is utilized to make proteins. Proteins are one of the primary nutritional categories alongside fats and sugars. Not at all like fats and starches, which just contain carbon, hydrogen and oxygen, proteins contain nitrogen notwithstanding these three components. Proteins are viewed as building squares of life. Keeping in mind the end goal to supply this basic component, manures are rich in nitrogen.

Sorts of compost

Manures could be in strong shape or fluid. The sort of compost required for your harvests relies upon the kind of plants you have planted. This is because of the way that each plant has its own particular requirements for various substances that are fundamental for its development. The Specific supplements contained in a compost additionally decide its classification.

Supplement substance

Since various components are required for solid development of plants, composts are rich in them. These components include:

1. Nitrogen

Nitrogen is the most essential of these since it is utilized to make proteins. Proteins are one of the principle nutrition types alongside fats and starches. Not at all like fats and sugars, which just contain carbon, hydrogen and oxygen, proteins contain nitrogen notwithstanding these three components. Proteins are viewed as building pieces of life. Keeping in mind the end goal to supply this basic component, manures are rich in nitrogen, which is more often than not around half. This basically appears as nitrate mixes.

2. Potassium

The most well-known wellspring of this fundamental component in manures is potassium nitrate. Potassium is required by the plant for legitimate use of water.

3. Phosphorus

This component is an unquestionable requirement for plant development. While it is generally provided in huge sums, over measurement could hamper the dissolvability of different supplements required by plants. Phosphorus is typically included the type of super phosphate or phosphoric corrosive.

Notwithstanding the previously mentioned, different supplements like iron, magnesium, sulfur, zinc, copper, calcium, potassium, chloride and so forth are additionally required. These could be provided either through the development medium, or by supplemental application.

The measure of the supplements being provided must be precisely observed. Just by appropriate application would optimum be able to plant development be achieved which would at last prompt a decent collect and high benefits.

Chapter 30 - Warming Up A Greenhouse

Certain geological areas encounter climatic extremes as far as temperature. In these conditions, numerous plant species can't survive, inciting agriculturists to rehearse trim turn. Therefore, crops show up in the market amid particular seasons. Since there is interest for money trims consistently, a lot of yields must be foreign made and transported from other climatic areas, prompting ascend in costs amid offseason. In any case, to beat this issue, scientists have thought of developing them in Greenhouses outfitted with warmers. In any case, warmers are costly gadgets and one must pick the best alternative accessible, contingent on the sort of yield, the particular prerequisites of the product and the climate states of the area.

Greenhouse warmers commonly utilize 1.8-4.8 Watts of vitality, contingent on the volume of air being warmed inside the Greenhouse. For bigger estimated Greenhouses, a few warmers might be required. Be that as it may, the higher cost amid off seasons is probably going to counterbalance their running expense. Besides, these items would positively contend well against imported ones, since they are probably going to be new items than their transported in partners, which for the most part make a trip long separations to achieve the market.

Kinds of Greenhouse radiators

There are different kinds of Greenhouse radiators that are appropriate for Greenhouse. They are for the most part arranged in view of the sort of fuel they devour. While obtaining a radiator, you should make sure there is prepared access to the kind of information your chose warmer requires. In light of the paradigm of fuel compose, the different choices accessible include:

1. Electric radiators

These radiators are most appropriate for beginner specialists since they don't release effluents and are purpose to utilize notwithstanding when left unmonitored amid evening time. Besides, they are not massive, and a be introduced on the ground or can suspended from the roof.

2. Gas warmers

These warmers are filled by flammable gas propane. Since pipe gas is created from them, legitimate ventilation is required for finish ignition. Without appropriate ventilation, their utilization can be unsafe since fragmented ignition produces carbon monoxide, which is toxic for the two people and plants. These radiators can be exorbitant in the event that you don't have a shoddy wellspring of gaseous petrol in your Greenhouse.

3. Paraffin warmers

As on account of gas warmers, paraffin radiators emanate smoke and in this manner require a smoke stack. They additionally require a dependable wellspring of fuel for their task to be prudent.

4. Coal warmers

Like other non-sustainable fuel radiators, these warmers require a solid supply of coal to proceed with task, and additionally appropriate ventilation for air supply and ejection of pipe gases.

Essential thought

For a radiator to be viable, the Greenhouse must be appropriately protected for the warmth to stay inside its nook. While 100% protection is unthinkable, endeavors must be made to limit warm misfortune, generally the cost of fuel is probably going to disintegrate the gainfulness of your wander. For best outcomes, the master exhort must be looked for to gain the most appropriate radiator for your Greenhouse. Since it is a noteworthy speculation, appropriate homework must be done before making the buy.

Chapter 31 - Keeping up Humidity Levels Inside A Greenhouse

Plants require water and daylight and carbon dioxide to fabricate their sustenance. This is refined through a procedure called photosynthesis. Without the nearness of the three previously mentioned operators, photosynthesis seizes to happen. Therefore the plant starves and kicks the bucket. While it is imperative to water plants routinely, it is additionally basic to keep up the ideal level of dampness in the climate for the plants' prosperity. The significance of dampness can be checked through a comprehension of the procedure of transpiration.

Transpiration

Plants retain water from their underlying foundations. This water is transported by the procedure of osmosis to specific tissues, known as xylem, which spend significant time in transporting water as far as possible up to the takes off. It is basically in the leaves that the procedure of photosynthesis happens. Notwithstanding water, the basic supplements required by plants are likewise conveyed to the leaves, disintegrated in water. From the leaves, overabundance water is discharged into the air as water vapors. The dissipation of water has a critical impact in keeping the plants cool. It additionally serves to transport supplements up to the leaves, since without dissipation, leaves would get water logged, whereby the xylem tissues will get immersed and no further retention of water will be conceivable by the roots. This procedure of transporting water from the roots to the leaves and its consequent discharge into the air is called transpiration.

For the procedure of transpiration to happen easily, the level of stickiness in air must be at an ideal level. On the off chance that there is abundance moistness, water won't vanish in leaves, along these lines making a condition where leaves get over doused. Therefore, the supply of supplements to the leaves gets ended. Despite what might be expected, if the level of dampness dips under ordinary, exorbitant dissipation will happen, soaking the leaves with supplement salts, and in addition exhausting water level in the dirt. A completely developed tree may lose a few hundred liters of water through its leaves in hot and dry conditions. Around 90% of the water that is consumed by the plant's foundations is spent in this procedure. Without water, plant will be not able combine their nourishment and will starve. Besides, inordinate transpiration will likewise drop their temperature beneath typical.

Keeping up mugginess inside the Greenhouse

Evaporative coolers can help in keeping up temperature and in addition stickiness inside a Greenhouse. Different units are accessible that bundle warmers and humidifiers to keep up temperature and stickiness. Humidifiers can viably control dampness level in air. Different contraptions that go with humidifiers are directional wind current louvers, which keep up stream of air, along these lines humidifying, ventilating, and cooling the atmosphere inside the Greenhouse.

Coolers accessible industrially are intended to suite their motivation in a Greenhouse. A few models have overwhelming measure, zinc-covered metallic louvers and cupboards including zinc-chromate.

The measure of daylight got by plants relies upon regular climatic conditions. Over introduction to the sun can happen amid summers. It is prudent to introduce cooling and humidifying frameworks to keep up the correct temperature in the Greenhouse. This utility reaches out amid the winter season, when daylight could be rare.

Legitimate warming and ventilation in a Greenhouse is critical to develop sound plants and fitting frameworks must be introduced to keep up temperature and mugginess at ideal levels.

Chapter 32 - 5 Factors To Consider When Choosing Greenhouse Lighting

In basic terms, a Greenhouse is intended to develop plants in a controlled domain that furnishes them with ideal conditions required for their prosperity. This basically implies plants are never again developing in open nature, however inside secured fenced in areas. The individual in charge of the Greenhouse should subsequently guarantee that plants are given reasonable conditions like the ones delighted in by their partners developing in nature.

Light

Plants make their nourishment by the procedure of photosynthesis. In nature, this procedure devours daylight, water and carbon dioxide to make sugars and other natural exacerbates that serve a nourishment and are basic for the development of plants. It is in this way imperative that plants get satisfactory daylight inside the Greenhouse. This is particularly the case in winters, when daylight is rare. It is here that utility of fake lights becomes an integral factor. Different diverse writes or manufactured lighting frameworks are accessible in the market today. Choosing a reasonable lighting framework can regardless demonstrate dubious, particularly for those new to them.

Variables to be considered when obtaining Greenhouse lighting

Before really purchasing a Greenhouse lighting framework, you should remember the accompanying contemplations in order to get the most appropriate light for your Greenhouse.

1. Sort of your Greenhouse

Before choosing the light, you should consider the sort of Greenhouse you will introduce it in. Regardless of whether it is a business or an individual Greenhouse. The sort of Greenhouse directs the kind of light that is most suited to it. For a business Greenhouse, the lighting framework must have the capacity to endure unfriendly working conditions that are normally found inside.

2. Working hours

The measure of light use in the Greenhouses depends on "photoperiods." Photoperiods are characterized as time interims amid which light will be exchanged on. The length of these photoperiods changes, contingent on the season, atmosphere and area of the Greenhouse. A photoperiod of 12 hours implies that in 24 hours of a day, lights may work for 12 hours.

It is thusly critical that the light bought will have the capacity to work for eras that are equivalent to the required photoperiods.

3. Reason

You should buy a lighting framework that will center around your necessities. In the event that you need to prompt development in blossoming plants, it is best to purchase a source that will discharge more "range hues" like red, blue and the "far-red wavelengths." The hues contained in the light being radiated have extensive impact on development of plants. This implies not all hues in the light range deliver the required impacts.

4. Electrical effectiveness

Lighting frameworks are quite often fueled by power. This implies working a lighting framework will add to your power bills. Electrical effectiveness can have a critical influence in decreasing your bills, while demonstrating a similar measure of glow.

5. Warmth

No light source is 100% productive. This implies some measure of electrical info will dependably be changed over into warm that will be produced by the light source. In such huge numbers of words, a light that is more a radiator than a light is no great. Overheating could really murder your plants.

Lighting is a critical parameter that contributes towards the advancement of a plant. It is along these lines critical to purchase the lighting framework that is most appropriate for your Greenhouse in order to guarantee solid development of your plants.

Chapter 33 - The Business Relationship Between Farmers And Greenhouse Manufacturers

As far back as cultivating developed ages prior, man has valued the significance of water system and daylight for reaping great yields. Close by, since old circumstances issues postured by terrible climate, plant infections and irritations have likewise existed. Subsequently, researchers and agriculturists have created composts, pesticides and herbicides to guarantee a fruitful yield.

While at first, the utilization of counterfeit manures and synthetic pesticide and herbicide showed enhanced yields, in the more extended run their destructive impacts began to raise issues. Thus, agriculturists and researcher propose to go return to natural cultivating hones.

The advantages of Greenhouses

Greenhouse offer an answer for securing crops against the antagonistic atmosphere and vermin, by giving a shut situation where plants can develop during the time without being assaulted by nuisances and plant illnesses.

Development of a Greenhouse

Greenhouses are generally developed utilizing a wooden or metallic system over which glass boards are laid to separate the inside from the outside condition. However this straightforward structure may not be sufficient to withstand unfavorable climate, bugs and plant ailments, and also corruption of the structure itself. Makers have in this manner think of inventive models utilizing new materials.

Greenhouse casings would now be able to be manufactured from aluminum or plastic individuals, which are rust and also termite safe. Boards used to cover structure can on the other hand be made of plastic or film. These materials are smash confirmation as against glass and along these lines ready to withstand overwhelming snow and hail storms. Besides, these materials are scratch verification and can support affect from even from a stone is flung at the board. Moreover, as contrasted and glass, these materials are known offer better security against bright beams from the sun. Bright or UV beams are outstanding malignancy specialists and are destructive to the two plants and people. The development of a Greenhouse at last relies upon the prerequisites of the cultivator and the zone accessible for the reason.

The part of Greenhouse producers

Greenhouse producers, notwithstanding making covers for the plants, likewise give instruments and devices That assistance in keeping up a great domain expected to manage plant development. Ranchers who develop trims in chilly areas require radiators that would keep plants warm amid cool spells. Producers can likewise supply clocks that supply water discontinuously amid the day so plants can retain water and supplements that are required for legitimate development.

Producers who have worked together finished years can offer valuable exhortation concerning establishment, and authorizing of the Greenhouse, the best possible hardware it should be furnished with. They can likewise familiarize the rancher with creative cultivating procedures like hydroponics.

Utilizing water as the development medium rather than soil, this procedure is known to anticipate plant ailments and nuisances, accordingly expanding profitability by 4-6 times.

Numerous producers likewise offer to introduce and commission the Greenhouse inside guarantee. This is offer especially helpful since Greenhouses are overwhelming and contain things that are sensitive to deal with. Harmed gear is typically expensive for the agriculturist to supplant.

Cooperating with Greenhouse producers would empower agriculturists to upgrade their returns consequently expanding their benefits. Moreover, natural products, vegetables and blossoms would be accessible in the market all the year round.

Chapter 34 - Distinguishing The Best Greenhouse Manufacturer

A great many people are mark cognizant with regards to purchasing an item. The brand really gives a thought regarding the nature of that specific item. Makers thusly attempt to keep up the nature of that standard since they remain to lose their market in the event that they trade off the quality.

Like different items you should consider the producer and the brand when you purchase a Greenhouse. The majority of the Greenhouses accessible can be purchased off the rack as units. Others are accessible in gathered frame or exceptionally developed models. It is vital that you are certain of the nature of segments that are utilized as a part of making the Greenhouse.

While thinking about various makers, one must remember the accompanying focuses to strike a decent arrangement.

1. Get your work done

before going for the buy, you should distinguish your particular prerequisites that relate to the region you intend to introduce your hot house in, and the kind of plants you are anticipating develop. A brand known to create great outcomes in some territory or for a specific sort of yield may not be reasonable in your area or for your harvests. It is along these lines prudent look for counsel from individuals who are as of now occupied with Greenhouse organizations.

2. Know the maker

Subsequent to recognizing an appropriate Greenhouse for yourself, The best activity is to keep an eye on its producer. An apparently garish item does not naturally ensure great quality. Such a check can regularly affirm the nature of the Greenhouse you have picked. A decent producer normally ensures consumer loyalty. Therefore, you consequently get safeguarded against glitches and quality related imperfections.

3. Accreditations

It is insightful to check with the producer on the off chance that it is partnered with a presumed affiliation. In the event that you purchase a Greenhouse from a maker associated with such a body, you would make certain that managing a dependable organization.

Besides, you should ensure you purchase your Greenhouse from a producer who executes worldwide quality and ,material models, for example, the ISO 9000 and ASTM gauges while making the item.

4. Glance around

Going inside and out for the main producer that you go over is never prescribed, even it is an exceedingly respectable organization. It is smarter to glance around for additional. Along these lines you will get an opportunity to do a market overview that will empower you communicate with various makers or their specialists, think about costs of various brands and parts and distinguish diverse alternatives that are industrially accessible.

The best deal may not depend totally on the notoriety and aptitude of the maker. The cost paid for the item is likewise a main consideration in getting a reasonable arrangement. Moreover, most new participants in the market offer items that are quality confirmed and tantamount to existing business sector pioneers at a less expensive cost.

5. The web

On the web, one gets a colossal assortment of brands to assess and look over. On the off chance that there are very few sellers in your region or you cannot manage the cost of the opportunity to really do a physical market review, at that point web is the appropriate response. Over the web, you get the opportunity to assess the brand without much trouble. Moreover, an online study additionally has the benefit of getting to surveys gave by purchasers themselves.

Choosing the most reasonable Greenhouse producer can turn out to be exceptionally difficult. Be that as it may, by the day's end you get its advantage in wording your own fulfillment.

Chapter 35 - Framing Up The Greenhouse

Over the globe, as far back as the approach of human progress, man has developed yields in the open condition. Indeed, even today, a large portion of the manors remain in outdoors. Notwithstanding, in the open condition, powers of nature can not be controlled. This is the motivation behind why a few ranchers choose Greenhouses where conditions can be successfully observed to suit the plants' needs.

The Greenhouse is a blend of a casing with boards introduced over it. The casing gives the fundamental structure of the Greenhouse while boards shape the rooftop and dividers of Greenhouse. Boards are composed let in daylight to keep the plants warm for most extreme development. They do this by catching the warmth from the sun inside itself. In the event that the plants inside don't require a ton of daylight, boards can be secured with dark spreads to piece abundance daylight from entering the walled in area.

Before, Greenhouse boards were produced using glass. Since glass isn't smash verification, it is powerless amid hailstorms and substantial snowfall. These days, substitute materials such an acrylic or plastic are accessible, which are shatterproof.

Kinds of boards accessible in the market

There are three kinds of boards promptly accessible in the market.

1. Glass

The most widely recognized material used to make Greenhouse boards is glass. Normal glass does not give insurance against bright beams from the sun, exorbitant presentation to which can be hindering to plants. Moreover, since normal glass is inclined to break, treated glass which is more grounded than customary glass is regularly utilized as a substitute. A respectable contractual worker must be procured to introduce glass boards in light of their weight and delicacy.

2. Plastic

Plastic boards can be produced using fiberglass, polyester, acrylic or polycarbonate. These materials can withstand affect from hails, substantial snowfall, balls and shakes. Likewise, plastic boards are lightweight and enable ideal measure of daylight to enter the Greenhouse.

3. Film boards

This compose utilizes a film that is extended over the board. Typically, polyethylene and polyester films are utilized as a part of Greenhouse boards. These boards offer sufficient assurance from the sun. In addition, these boards are prudent and can be acquired as rolls.

Picking the board most appropriate for you

Each of the previously mentioned boards accompanies its points of interest and burdens. Picking the correct sort will relies upon the use of the Greenhouse and the sorts of plants that would be developed inside. Having the most appropriate boards will guarantee that plants would have the capacity to become round the year.

Boards can either be obtained from the merchant or be uniquely designed to fit the Greenhouse. Both cultivator and the contractual worker should quantify the site before the boards are made in order to guarantee appropriate size. In the event that enlisting a contractual worker is past the rancher's financial plan, certain sites on the web that offer administrations at a lower cost could be investigated.

Plants produce their sustenance by the procedure of photosynthesis. In nature, this procedure devours daylight, water and carbon dioxide to make sugars and other natural intensifies that serve a nourishment and are fundamental for the development of plants. It is in this way vital that plants get satisfactory daylight inside the Greenhouse. This is particularly the case in winters, when daylight is rare. It is hence vital that the correct sort of boards are introduced, which will enable plentiful measure of light to achieve plants, while securing them against the unsafe bright radiation show in sun beams.

Chapter 36 - Picking And Comparing Greenhouse Panels

Boards frame the dividers and roof of your Greenhouse. Keeping in mind the end goal to empower the Greenhouse to really have the capacity to hold warm inside its limits, these boards must have the capacity to protect its walled in area from the outside environment. Along these lines, warming expenses can be kept inside sensible cutoff points.

People looking to introduce a Greenhouse as an interest, must think about the properties of the board material and check whether it acclimates with the necessities of the plants that are to be developed in the Greenhouse. It is additionally fitting to go for an insulative and flame resistant board.

Different materials are accessible for Greenhouse boards, with every material having its advantages and disadvantages. Glass, fiberglass, and polycarbonates, are more qualified for a Greenhouse specialist. Plastic boards, then again are more prevalent with business Greenhouses administrators. Plastic boards, be that as it may, are not especially sturdy and require visit substitution.

Glass boards

Glass framing extremely appealing in appearance. They are additionally simple to keep up since they are less defenseless against scratches. They additionally have a long life unless subjected to affect that could smash the glass. Glass framing is a decent decision from tasteful perspective. Notwithstanding giving your Greenhouse a lovely viewpoint, glass boards transmit a lot of light into the Greenhouse.

The thickness of glass, then again, is very high as contrasted and other board materials. On the off chance that glass boards are chosen, the establishment and encircling must be sufficiently solid to support its weight. Additionally, since glass is delicate and substantial, it is very costly to introduce glass boards. In such manner, proficient help must be looked for and mind must be taken to avoid individual damage and also material harm.

Polycarbonate

While polycarbonate boards are not as engaging as their glass partners, they are more sturdy. Moreover, their insulative properties are likewise very great, particularly when utilized as a part of a twofold or triple sheet arrangement. This empowers the Greenhouse to contain more warmth inside, along these lines decreasing warming expenses. In any case, contrasted and glass, polycarbonate needs straightforwardness. Subsequently, daylight let in through these boards isn't as exceptional as for the situation with glass.

Fiberglass

Boards produced using fiberglass are solid, lightweight and break verification. Be that as it may, a great quality fiberglass must be chosen for the boards as a less than stellar score is probably going to stain, in this manner lessening light entrance with time.

The gum covering present on account of fiberglass in the end wears off, making soil amass between the strands. Hence, another sap covering must be connected after around 15 years. While at first the straightforwardness is practically identical with that of glass, it lessens with time, particularly on account of low quality fiberglass.

Plastic boards

Both polycarbonate or acrylic plastic, have warm sparing and also long-life traits.

While acrylic does not stain, polycarbonate for the most part turns yellow. The two materials are generally ensured for straightforwardness for up to10 years. These materials likewise have leeway of being reasonable for bended surfaces-polycarbonate being most bendable of the two materials.

The most appropriate board material relies upon your necessities and in addition the conditions that win in your area. In such manner, you should likewise remember your budgetary obliges. This best arrangement would just be the one that your pocket permits. the one that your pocket permits.

Chapter 37 - Picking A Window Greenhouse

Winter season can regularly be desolate and discouraging, particularly in the event that you watch out of your window, just to discover defoliated plants and chilly, dead flowerbeds. In the relatively recent past, these dormant flowerbeds would have been secured with a wide range of brilliant and appealing blossoms. Be that as it may, by utilizing the idea of a window Greenhouse, one can change the dull standpoint of your window into one showing a wide range of bright plants.

A window Greenhouse can likewise locate its utility with plant darlings with restricted space. A window Greenhouse, likewise called a garden window, has a little development. Utilizing this little garden you can appreciate see blooms bloom all round the year.

Before acquiring your garden window, factors, for example, cost, materials and the span of your window must be considered.

In the market, finish cove window packs are accessible that are both vitality productive and simple to introduce. Moreover, these window Greenhouses fill another need that is to expand the profundity or "open up" your room.

Sorts of Greenhouse windows

For the most part two kinds of window Greenhouses are promptly accessible for you to browse. These are bow Greenhouse windows and sound Greenhouse windows.

A bow write window Greenhouse involves a few glass sections give it an adjusted look. Then again, sound Greenhouse windows more often than not has three sections, whereby sides are calculated at 30 or 45 degrees.

Of the different alternatives accessible to you, the most conservative choice is use an entire pack of a bow-type Greenhouse as opposed to building another Greenhouse yourself. For this situation, you should simply to expel the current window in your room, amplify the opening as per the size specified in the manual and after that basically introduce the Greenhouse set up.

It is astute to buy a pack that matches the extent of your current window, so extra work required with growth of the opening can be limited. Besides, the size should likewise suit the plants that would populate your Greenhouse. First of all, a littler window Greenhouse unit would be a superior alternative. However for more open space you ought to go for a unit that offers more noteworthy profundity.

Bow Greenhouse windows produced using vinyl or aluminum covered wood are very alluring. The inside is produced using regular wood or impersonation wood. Typically recolored or painted vinyl gives a genuine look and has the benefit of being without upkeep.

While settling on a choice to buy Greenhouse you should choose a protected bow compose Greenhouse window. The glass framing ought to be produced using glass that has protecting spacer.

Situation

So as to choose the best area, overview your home for the area having "instant" characteristics that help your window Greenhouse. These characteristics incorporate warmth, sufficient daylight and water get to. In addition, the area must be to such an extent that you have simple access to it, without making block different exercises in your home.

It is a smart thought to purchase window boxes and orchestrate them inside your Greenhouse. Along these lines, you appreciate summer blooms amid fall by planting them these pots. Herbs could be a helpful expansion to your Greenhouse window as they are alluring, valuable and fragrant.

By having a Greenhouse window, you would now be able to have the joy of cultivating throughout the entire year, regardless of what sort of climate wins outside.

Chapter 38 - Appreciating Greenhouse Gardening

Individuals invest their free energy as indicated by their interests. Some bustling themselves with sports while others like culinary. Individuals who cherish plants appreciate cultivating. With the correct sort of instruments and hardware, plant sweethearts can embellish their home while making the most of their pastime.

The interest of dealing with plants requires that you invest very some energy with you plants, watering them, keeping nuisances from hurting them and expelling weeds from your plants' region. Be that as it may, these exercises could open you to the sun for expanded periods, causing sunburns. An elective alternative that will shield you from over dosage of daylight, without bargaining on your pastime is to have a Greenhouse.

Development of a Greenhouse

A Greenhouse is an encased structure that houses plants inside a controlled mood for them to thrive. Its development contains a system with boards put on the edge. The edge is produced using either wood or metal. Then again, Greenhouse boards, which shape the dividers and roof of the Greenhouse, are produced using glass or plastic. A run of the mill Greenhouse is a detached structure. Be that as it may, if very little space is accessible, at that point influencing a connection to your home to can do the trap. For this situation, your Greenhouse would basically be an extra room in your home.

Before you set out after developing the Greenhouse, it is valuable to check if conforms to the construction laws your territory. In basic words, you should be permitted to fabricate your picked outline by the experts. Choosing the area of your Greenhouse is essential and is directed by the atmosphere of your area. On the off chance that it gets exceptionally sweltering amid summer you may get a kick out of the chance to construct the Greenhouse under a tree for shade.

Developing a Greenhouse can be very costly. On the off chance that purchasing a Greenhouse pack, or having a temporary worker fabricate one or you is past your methods, it would be a smart thought to set one up starting with no outside help. In the wake of doing the fundamental printed material, you can begin building one immediately.

Post development issues

When you have a Greenhouse, picking the plants to develop in your Greenhouse is the subsequent stage. This progression requires some exploration. In such manner, one may jump at the chance to counsel the web or visit the neighborhood planting shop to complete a review.

The vast majority utilize Greenhouses to developing blooming plants. This pattern is presently being supplanted with being used for foods grown from the ground so that these can be made accessible everywhere throughout the year. Moreover, cultivating strategies are currently being executed into planting .subsequently, soil isn't generally utilized as a development medium. Be that as it may, water can likewise be utilized rather than soil. This strategy is called hydroponics which basically dispenses with the issue of weeds, in this manner sparing a considerable measure of time and bother.

The diversion of developing plants in a Greenhouse can even reward you with attractive benefits. Since the Greenhouse empowers you to develop foods grown from the ground all around the year, you could really auction your deliver amid seasons, when costs are high. For this reason, you should simply to offer your collect in a neighborhood market.

Before setting up a Greenhouse you should complete a careful research and know about your budgetary points of confinement. Along these lines you will have the capacity to stay away from issues and will really make the most of your side interest.

Chapter 39 - Building An Easy And Cost-compelling Greenhouse On Your Back Yard

Preceding setting out on your Greenhouse venture, you should do appropriate arranging as this would spare a ton of problem and additionally cash. The outline of your green would rely upon your home's engineering, space, the plants that you intend to develop and the accessible spending plan. The Greenhouse must have the capacity to give an appropriate situation to the plants it is proposed for.

Area

Since plants produce their sustenance by utilizing vitality from daylight, it is fundamental that the Greenhouse is found to such an extent that it gets adequate measure of daylight. An excess of daylight, however can be pernicious for plants. With a specific end goal to shield it from high force light, tree shade can turn out to be very useful. Deciduous trees, for example, oak and maple can give satisfactory shade over a Greenhouse along these lines shielding its inhabitants from solid late evening sun in summers. In any case, the area must be arranged with the end goal that the shade does not piece daylight toward the beginning of the day. Deciduous trees, not at all like coniferous or other evergreen trees, consequently allow daylight amid winters, since they defoliate in that season. Evergreen trees are in this way not desirable over sanctuary Greenhouses.

The site you intend to erect your Greenhouse on must have great seepage. This can be accomplished by developing it on high ground. Inappropriate waste will cause water logging, which make plants rot.

Development

To build a Greenhouse for your home, you would require a sheet of Universal Canopy, around 10 x 20 feet in estimate. You would likewise require 6 mil clear plastic move, around 20 x 100 feet in measure, 4 to 8 T-Posts, 15 to 20 Squeeze Clips, 18 Ratcheting Tie-downs, 1 move duck tape, 3 moves Heavy Duty 3M Clear Tape. You could likewise incorporate warmers, fans, and gro-lights as a choice.

When you have the previously mentioned stuff, you could continue by following the rule given beneath:

1. First of all, set up your casing, and as you embed each piece wrap the association point with 2 or 3 rounds of Duck Tape.

2. Next, connect the Tie downs by amazing every one of them equally finished the highest point of the casing. Make the ties tight, however don't exposed down and over fix.

3. Use no less than 4 T-post to stay the 4 corners of the Greenhouse. Place the T-post within a drive no less than 12" in the ground. at that point wrap in any event the best 24" with Duck Tape to secure and wipe out any sharp edges.

4.   Now join two sheets of plastic with a specific end goal to accomplish full scope. (unless you discovered greater plastic) Cut 2 bits of plastic at 30 feet. this will give both of you, 20' x 30' pieces. You will graft the 30' segments, giving you one major sheet of 38' x 30'.

5.   Allow the plastic to touch the ground on the end tops, however in the event that your cover was to much and it won't achieve the ground on the two finishes. In any case you can make your own particular end tops or entryways with the additional plastic.

6.   Use the clasps to join the plastic to the pipe legs. Clasp wherever you think it needs it. Any tears caused by the clasps can be settled with obligational clear tape.

When you have effectively taken after all the previously mentioned advances you have developed your own special Greenhouse. Congrats!

Chapter 40 - Greenhouses On The Move

Greenhouses are quick getting to be noticeably well known with plant darlings. Due to the advantages a Greenhouse brings to the table, an ever-increasing number of specialists are thinking about on having one in their homes. In any case, a great many people are likely change habitation for various reasons, including better openings for work. Since a full-sized Greenhouses would be unfeasible to move, such individuals can make utilization of versatile kinds.

Convenient Greenhouses, are required to be light weight with the goal that they are anything but difficult to exchange. Besides, they should be minimal, east to setup and destroy. Truth be told most compact Greenhouse units can be raised within 30 minutes. Being smaller, these Greenhouses can be effortlessly put away in a helpful area, for example, a carport or in a storage room when not in utilized.

Reason

Regarding usefulness, compact Greenhouses are required to trap daylight inside their walled in area, making utilization of the Greenhouse impact. This is precisely what is expected of a normal Greenhouse. Be that as it may, notwithstanding this a convenient Greenhouse is required to be light weight and simple to commission.

Convenience

Compact Greenhouses are appropriate for early ranch of seeds, insurance of delicate plants from cool climate and developing distinctive plants species not generally found in the territory.

Ubiquity

The ubiquity of compact Greenhouses in on the ascent among Greenhouse workers. This is essentially because of the way that these models set up rapidly and effortlessly. Moreover, they can be pulled down inside no time, enabling the space to be utilized for some other reason. Consequently the space involved by a compact Greenhouse does not get bolted up, but rather stays accessible.

Convenient Greenhouses are additionally suggested for amateurs since this will permit them hands on understanding on a Greenhouse before they choose to construct a full-sized one. To top everything, versatile Greenhouses are modest to setup and also to keep up. Thus, beginners can start their planting without spending substantial wholes of cash to buy parts expected to setup a full-scale Greenhouse. Besides, since their establishment is speedier and less demanding than consistent ones so no propelled instruments or aptitude is required.

Kinds of versatile Greenhouses

Compact Greenhouses are accessible in different shapes and sizes. They could be as a little tent in which just 2 plant racks can be put.

Others may look like compact storerooms, around 6 feet tall. Greater models, around 7 to 8 feet high are likewise accessible. These bigger Greenhouses can suit up to 3 to 4 bigger retires inside.

Working a convenient Greenhouse

Climate conditions can vacillate quickly. Watch out for the climate report that is accessible on the web or communicate on your nearby radio and TV. Amid sudden chilly spells cover the Greenhouse during the evening with leaves filled sacks for protection. This would keep the vibe inside from getting icy. .

Amid hot spells, then again, the versatile Greenhouse can be moved to a shady area. On the other hand, some type of covering can be utilized over the casing to keep daylight from being transmitted inside.

Versatile Greenhouses would be helpful for both beginner plant specialists and in addition proficient ones. Their conveyability enables you to transport it to a more helpful area. Besides, Its upkeep isn't as exorbitant as for the situation with changeless, full-sized ones. Subsequently, every one stands to profit by a compact Greenhouse.

Thanks again for buying my book. If you have a minute, please leave a positive review. You can leave your review by clicking on this link:

Leave your review here. Thank you!

I take reviews seriously and always look at them. This way, you are helping me provide you better content that you will LOVE in the future. A review doesn't have to be long, just one or two sentences and a number of stars you find appropriate (hopefully 5 of course).

Also, if I think your review is useful, I will mark it as "helpful." This will help you become more known on Amazon as a decent reviewer, and will ensure that more authors will contact you with free e-books in the future. This is how we can help each other.

DISCLAIMER: This information is provided "as is." The author, publishers and/or marketers of this information disclaim any loss or liability, either directly or indirectly as a consequence of applying the information presented herein, or in regard to the use and application of said information. No guarantee is given, either expressed or implied, in regard to the merchantability, accuracy, or acceptability of the information. The pages within this e-book have been copyrighted.

www.ingramcontent.com/pod-product-compliance
Lightning Source LLC
LaVergne TN
LVHW010203070225
803196LV00007B/259